THE GUIDE TO
A LIFE WORTH LIVING

Encouraging, Soothing, and Inspiring
Wisdom for Your Inner Journey

NINA SKARPSNO HEIDE

Cover design: Laura Duffy
Interior design: KUHN Design Group

Book cover photo by Simon Dannhauer.
Serengetti National Park, Tanzania, Africa

Find the book on:

WWW.A-LIFE-WORTH-LIVING.ORG

*To my two beautiful sons and
my loving husband.*

CONTENTS

• • •

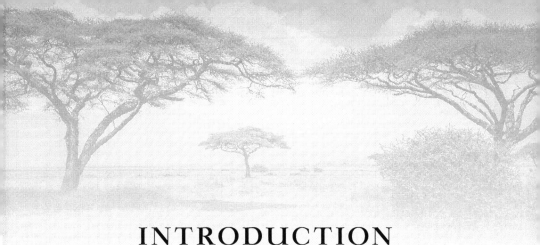

INTRODUCTION

We live in a time where many feel paralysed by unrest and crises, both internal and external. You may be in a difficult situation yourself, and perhaps you doubt whether you can fulfil your dreams. The good news is, if you really want to reach for your goals and change your life for the better, you just need to be willing to clean up your thought patterns and choose to think more consciously.

A new focus and more conscious thoughts will enable you to create a life that feels exciting, good and meaningful. Before you spend time on this book, ask yourself if you are interested in devoting twenty minutes of each day to learning to focus your mind.

You might think, "Sure, everybody would sacrifice a few minutes a day to create a life that feels good and is really worth living." The truth is that very few people are willing to do this, not even if their lives feel like a slow death. It's so easy to find all kinds of excuses.

The main reason for unconscious living, though, is that we don't really believe in our own inner power. We might not know where to go with our lives, or at least not how to get there, and we are often too scared or indifferent to find out. A few people, however, have a strong longing to create their dreams. Are you one of them?

If you have the courage to change, let's start our journey towards conscious living together.

> Before we begin our journey, I want to make you aware of the website and the forum that complement this guide. On the forum, you can communicate with like-minded people. You can also join contests to find solutions on global issues. The website has a "Feel Good" page where you can listen to the people I refer to in this book. In addition, the website includes my blog, great music, meditations, inspirational videos, fun stuff and much more. Enjoy! **www.a-life-worth-living.org**

BACKGROUND STORY

My name is Nina Skarpsno Heide. I'm from Stavanger, Norway; however, I've lived more than twenty years of my life in Africa, first working for the UN and later working for NGOs with the mission of helping street children towards dignity.

I will begin this guide by telling you why I personally decided to go on a journey towards conscious living and, as a result, ended up writing this book.

In January 2004, my children and I moved back from Kampala to Stavanger. This was eight months before my husband's contract was finished in Foreign Affairs. Our house needed renovating, and I knew it could take time to get a job and settle in. Moving back to Norway without my husband ended up being much, much harder than I believed was possible, and, as a result, I got sick. Soon after, I was diagnosed with diabetes type 1 (LADA).

At first, the disease was very difficult to manage. I was taking insulin injections, but my body was still producing some insulin. The result was severe blood sugar fluctuations that eventually led to fatigue, anxiety and depression. While my previous life was exciting, now my life felt like a nightmare.

When I became ill, I had no idea how to use my own thoughts and feelings to return to the life I wanted to live. Instead, I used my diabetes, anxiety, and exhaustion as excuses to stay depressed in bed.

What kept me in bed with depression was the thought of never again being able to do a job I was proud of. Ever since I was very young, I have wanted to make a difference in this world. But how was it possible to make a difference when I got exhausted just from taking a shower and then needed to go back to bed?

During the following years, I went through different doctors and therapists. Some good came out of it. However, it was only after I started listening to Esther and Abraham Hicks (my spiritual guides) that I really began to understand that I create my world through the way I choose to think.

I don't remember exactly how and when I started to listen to Esther and Abraham Hicks, but I do remember it was from that point that I began taking responsibility for my life. I realised that I was the only one who could make myself healthy, and I could only do so through changing my own thoughts and feelings.

Today I see that Esther and Abraham's teaching was right for me. I have now regained the spark of life and energy. I live the life I want to live, and I am able to work with the things that inspire me.

Slowly but surely, with my new toolbox, I have moved my life in the direction that gives me a sense of meaning. A meaningful life and feeling joy were two of the things I had on my wish list for the future.

I also gained relief from another problem. For a long time, even before I became ill, I felt claustrophobic when in dark places such as tunnels and caves. I felt anxious and often struggled to breathe. After working with my own thoughts and feelings, I realised that this was no longer the case. I can now even crawl quite a distance with my back scraping the roof of a pitch-black cave without a problem. That discovery proved to me that I had returned to a normal life – in fact, a life even better than normal.

Today, I'm extremely grateful for this challenging experience, as it forced me to make some important choices. Now life feels really good, and I believe I have the tools to handle whatever comes my way.

I hope my story might help others who are struggling, as I was, to find their way out of the dark. The idea of helping them face their challenges is another thought that brings me happiness.

My wish is to share some of the tools I picked up on my way so you can take a shortcut on your journey from fear to love, from sickness to health, from boredom to excitement, or whatever your starting and ending points might be. These tools are multipurpose; they make you confident and grateful, and take you wherever you want to go ...

Ready?

WHAT TO EXPECT...

I'll help you discover your dream life and make you conscious of what beliefs and values are preventing you from living that dream. You'll soon find out that the difficulties in reaching your dream are hidden within your thoughts and influenced by how you choose to think about yourself and the world around you.

You might not always agree with the way I have interpreted my life. However, the purpose of this journey is for you to find your own answers to the big questions in your life and use your conscious beliefs to move yourself forward.

I have chosen a spiritual angle for this guide. I did this because I quickly discovered that I could not get anywhere until I was willing to look closely at all the thoughts I have about myself and my life, including the spiritual ones.

By being willing to examine my existential beliefs, I discovered a great deal of fear, guilt and shame hidden in the depths of my emotions. Before I began my journey of consciousness, I had no idea how harmful these thoughts were to both my body and my mind. Only when I consciously chose to opt out of thoughts that undermined my ability to relax and feel good was I able to regain my energy and zest for life.

In this guide, therefore, I also share my spiritual thoughts with you. You don't have to adopt everything I have chosen to believe. Your task will be to actively choose to see life in a way that is right for you and that makes you personally feel good.

This journey of self-discovery is meant to be exciting, playful and fun and you'll learn to accept, respect and love yourself, others and your life.

How much you'll get out of it, though, depends on how open you are to change and how much focus you're willing to put into this life-changing experience.

You will need a journal for this work. I'll give you three assignments at the beginning of every month and you'll log the assignments in your journal to keep track of your growth. If you choose to work more intensively with the book, spend one week instead of one month on each chapter.

This journey requires you to take responsibility for your own life. By working yourself through your own challenges, you can make sure you are moving forward to a life that feels good.

If you find it hard to make this journey on your own, set up a group or use this program together with a coach or a mentor. (You can search for a mentor under "Forum for Change" on **www.a-life-worth-living.org**.)

By allowing a whole year for this process, you'll give yourself a chance to change. The progress will be gradual but sure. With practice, you will develop good routines that will help you to continue your growth long after you've finished reading this guide. It's possible to do the journey in a shorter time, of course, but I recommend you use at least three months if you want lasting benefits from the journey.

I'll start out by doing the assignments first, using my own life experience as an example. Then it's your turn. My story is there only as a starting point, because of course ultimately you need to create your own dream.

Before starting the assignments. It's a good idea to read the entire guide first so that you get an overview before you write your responses, but you can start thinking about your answers straight away.

If you wish to purchase the workbook specifically made for this guide, you can make your order at the website **www.a-life-worth-living.org**. The workbook breaks down each assignment into several short questions and will thus help you to work with the tasks in a more focused and structured way. It will also include some practical exercises that can be fun to do with others. In addition, pages of journal entry are made available.

If you *only* read the guide and do not spend time on the assignments, you'll still be able to get a new and better insight into your life. However, if you want to make a real change, you'll need to be willing to do the exercises.

In order to change and learn new skills, theoretical knowledge is not enough. We must also be willing to practise. It's through the practical exercises and assignments that you'll really learn to grasp life and bring lasting changes. However, there is nothing wrong with using your own workbook rather than the fully focused workbook that is specially made for this guide.

FIRST JOURNEY TOGETHER

THE STARTING POINT

During the first two months/weeks, you'll get to know yourself to find a base from which to make your leap. In the next nine journeys, you'll look into what you believe and how you can believe differently, as it's not what happens to us in our lives but how we react that matters. By the final month/week, you will be ready to work on your specific dream by using all the tools you have discovered while going on this journey.

Understanding how you can respond differently to things that happen to you means you can change your life from being painful or dull to exciting, fun and meaningful. However, this requires you to be truthful to yourself. You'll need to be willing to look at your own life to discover what isn't working and how you can make it function. It also requires you to be willing to evaluate your beliefs to choose the ones that build your self-worth and make you believe in your own power.

To become the creator of your own life, you will start this journey by learning more about who you are, why you are here, and what you want to make out of this life.

WHY ARE WE HERE?

To live a conscious life, you will have to be honest with yourself, asking questions and being willing to search for what makes you happy, not just adapting to what others tell you to believe and do.

Respecting others' opinions and beliefs and understanding that we don't have to fit into the same square box will set your soul free.

If the thought of climbing Mount Everest doesn't make you happy, you shouldn't do it. But if others find the idea exhilarating, persuading them not to climb the mountain either will make their lives miserable. Becoming conscious and living a happy, meaningful life means that you need to stop and ask yourself what it is that makes you feel good and then allow others to do the same.

To live a conscious life, we also need to be able to ask the big questions. If you haven't done this before, this is your opportunity. And if you find it irrelevant, at least use this chance to ask yourself, "How can I enjoy my ride and live a purposeful life if I don't know what on earth I'm doing here?"

I started asking the big questions very early in my life. Nevertheless, it took me decades of searching before I found answers that resonated with my inner being. Having said that, my answers might not resonate with your inner being, and that's OK. We don't need to agree on everything to be able to take this journey together.

It is important that we have an understanding of why we are here so that, when life sucks, we know why and how we can turn our situation around to feel better. If you are afraid that this journey might interfere with your religion, don't worry. I'm not here to preach; believe what you want as long as it makes you feel good. However, it might be useful for you to know where I stand.

MY BELIEF

I never felt at home in our church. This was partly because the church never gave satisfactory answers to my questions about life, but it was also because I felt uncomfortable with the language of sinners and Hell, which hampered me in my need for feeling good.

What comforts me though, is to believe that I'm part of the Source, and that I'm here to learn to create and help expand the universe. Expanding the universe might sound a bit pretentious, but the universe is always growing, with or without our help.

To me, life feels much more purposeful and interesting if I can believe that I'm an important part of this big creation; at least, it makes me very happy to believe so. And as far as I have figured out, to be happy must be the purpose of our lives... or... what do you think? Isn't that what we all are striving for?

However, if we believe that we are sinners, that we don't matter or that we will be sent to Hell, then, in my opinion, life has no meaning. Becoming aware of what you want to believe about yourself and your life is therefore essential for this journey. This guide is nevertheless not intended to make anyone change their religion, but rather to provide insight into who we are and why we are here.

Without this insight, life can feel like a struggle. If life feels like agony, we will eventually stop dreaming. Even if we have a dream that we long for, our concerns and low energy levels will prevent us from focusing on the dream, as we have more than enough to deal with, handling all the problems of our daily lives. This is often the reason why we unconsciously choose to become "fire extinguishers," instead of people who consciously steer our lives in the direction we want to go.

Throughout this journey of consciousness, you will be able to learn to lift your focus from everyday challenges. As you begin to ask questions about life and become aware of what matters to you, you will find solutions and answers. When you begin to understand how life is really connected, life becomes easier and you will automatically start moving towards the life you dream about.

THE PURPOSE OF LIFE

What is the goal of your life? Have you ever sat down and thought carefully about what you want to get out of this lifetime?

Have you thought about why most of us want to find a partner, have children, get a good job, build a home, take vacations, learn new skills, help others, buy a car, get new haircuts, watch movies, shop, eat good food, visit friends, party, rest, travel and work out? I do these things because I believe they will make me happy and satisfied.

The vast majority of things you choose to do originate from your desire to feel happy and be satisfied so you can feel good. What makes me happy, however, might be very different from what makes you happy and content. But I believe that the goal of life, at least for the vast majority of us, is the desire to feel good.

But what would happen if you always felt happy and satisfied? Do you think you would see much change and expansion in your life if you were always satisfied? Ask yourself, "If I were happy in the comfort zone of my cave, would I make a lot of effort to learn new things, to see the world or to meet new people?" I really don't think so ... Do you?

As I see it, If we were always happy and content, we would not see any change in this world. So, if you wish to have the opportunity to develop, you actually need to feel a bit dissatisfied and sad in order to feel the pressure to change and seek new happiness.

Happiness is just a way of thinking, a choice, as it only requires that you consciously choose a better way of looking at a situation. However, you have to be conscious enough to be able to monitor your thoughts. When you forget to keep your head clear, it's very easy to see only the limitations of your situation. And be blind to all the possibilities your challenging situation can give you. You lose energy and feel unhappy and trapped when you don't see any solutions.

Nevertheless, none of us are perfect, as we are always changing and growing towards becoming improved versions of ourselves. With this view of life, **imperfection is actually perfect. If we could not change anything for the better, life would soon become boring, as we would not have any challenges and nothing to long for and work towards.**

The purpose of this self-awareness journey is to learn how to increase the amount of time you are conscious so that you feel good more often.

You might wonder why it is so important to feel good. It is because our dreams and goals always include the good feelings that we find at the top of our emotional scale, a place between satisfaction, hope,

happiness and freedom. To attract your dreams and live the life you long for, you need to find these feelings in the life you live here and now first. (I'll explain the idea of attraction later.)

On this self-development journey, you will therefore learn how to use different tools to train yourself to stay in the upper part of the emotion scale, so you can feel good more often. (See the scale below.)

Let's start with the soothing technique. This is a tool you can start using as soon as you notice your feelings are dropping. The soothing technique is actually so good that it is able to lift you from your heaviest and darkest feelings.

Every time you slip into the basement and feel fear, sadness or depression, this technique will help you to climb back to the top of your feelings, thus making sure you avoid spending too much time in the low vibrations, far away from the life you dream about. However, this requires that you remember to use the technique as soon as you feel down.

Most of us soothe ourselves, but few do it consciously, as we don't understand how effective soothing actually is in lifting our moods. You will now spend some time learning the importance of self-soothing and how you can practise this technique.

SOOTHING

Changing a feeling from fear to joy is not done in a single move. In any case, you'll need a bit of time; these feelings are far apart on the scale of emotions. However, it's not complicated; you just need practice. With practice, you'll soon be able to lift your emotions consciously and feel good.

Look at the scale below and find where your emotions are at this moment.

THE SCALE OF EMOTIONS:*

1. Joy/ knowledge/ inner strength/ freedom/ love/ gratitude

2. Passion

3. Enthusiasm/ happiness

4. Positive expectations/ faith

5. Optimism

6. Hope

7. Satisfaction

The feelings/emotions on top of the scale (from one to seven) are good and positive. Our goal is to learn to be up here as often as possible. Nevertheless, nobody manages to stay on top of the emotions scale all the time.

8. Boredom

9. Pessimism

10. Frustration/ irritation/ impatience

11. Overwhelm

The emotions from eight to eleven on the scale can be categorised as uncomfortable feelings. These are emotions that we can go in and out of several times a day. With the help of this guide, you can learn to lift yourself up from these feelings within seconds.

12. Disappointment

13. Doubt

14. Concern

---

* Esther and Abraham Hicks introduced me to the scale of emotions.

15. Disfavour

16. Discouragement

17. Anger

18. Vengefulness

19. Hate/ rage

20. Jealousy/ envy

21. Uncertainty/ guilt/ lack of self-worth

22. Fear/ sorrow/ depression/ despair/ powerlessness

At the bottom of the scale, we find the negative emotions. It may take longer to lift ourselves up from these emotions. However, with the soothing technique, you'll learn to lift yourself up from even the heaviest moods.

Your emotions might not be at the bottom of the scale; maybe you are just bored or pessimistic about your future, or you might be disappointed over something or someone in your life. Wherever you find yourself on the scale, if you're not at the top, there is always potential to feel better. Remember: your goal is just to move yourself up the scale one step at a time.

So let's try it out and start at the bottom:
If you feel **fear,** how can you move yourself up to feeling uncertain? What kind of words can you soothe yourself with?

An example of soothing words:
"It might not be as bad as I first believed."
"It could be worse."
"This will also pass."
"It will turn out OK at the end."
"To be able to feel joy, we need to feel down at times."

Your search for happy thoughts and feelings has a greater impact on your life than you might think. In fact, choosing good thoughts and feelings is the most important thing you can do.

This doesn't mean that you should not accept that you feel down or hurt sometimes. Rather the opposite. Accept that right now you are not feeling good, without blaming yourself or others. Nobody's feelings are on top all the time.

If you manage to comfort yourself by saying, "It's perfectly normal to feel down sometimes," you will soon notice that your self-comforting words are taking you up the emotional scale. If you get angry or disappointed with yourself or the people around you because you or they are not always on top, you may risk slipping completely into the basement of your emotions and then it will take much longer to recover. It is therefore important to know how you feel and remember to comfort yourself as soon as your feelings are on their way downhill.

Many of us are brought up believing that we are selfish if we think about our own well-being and put our own needs and feelings first. With this kind of belief, we could not be further from the truth. It's only through being responsible and taking care of our own needs and feelings that we can move ourselves forward.

If you don't take responsibility for how you feel, who will do it for you? Nobody can decide how other people should feel, but you can choose your own feelings.

If you try to relax and observe your feelings when you aren't feeling good, you will feel better much faster. In the same way, a parent may observe their child's emotional outburst without yelling, instead responding with loving words.

By comforting yourself and saying, "This will also pass," or "It might not be as bad as I first believed," you avoid becoming too disappointed, angry or depressed. In this way, you take responsibility for your emotions and prevent yourself from getting stuck in the basement of your own emotions.

You also determine your own development. Other people can't decide that you will learn from your mistakes or that you will seek change and expansion. Others can inspire you and cheer you up. However, without your own interest, family, friends and teachers can jump up and down or pull their hair out without you changing. The desire for change must therefore come from your own inner longing. If you are not willing to change, you will not be able to feel good.

If you do not develop yourself, you will feel stagnant, as everything around you is always in motion. Not following your own development is the same as trying to stop an unstoppable carousel from moving. You will feel pain every time you bump against the constantly moving carousel of growth. This will be the case until you decide to jump on the carousel and enjoy the ride towards inner growth and change.

THE UNIVERSAL GOAL

The reason why we feel pain when we refuse to move forward with our lives is that change is necessary if we want to grow and expand, and expansion and growth towards a loving, good and free world is the universal goal. Everything in this world is moving towards improvement, although it may not always look like that. I'll be talking more about this later.

Take some time to think through the next six paragraphs:

1. Everything you do starts with a thought. When you long for a better life, you help to grow and change your living conditions here on Earth and you become the creator of your own life.

2. When you change your thoughts and search for your own happiness, you are also changing the Earth. When consumed by dark thoughts, you may act accordingly, which can cause damage in your life and the lives of those around you. However, conscious thoughts will make you happy and, as the Earth is a part of the universe, your thoughts might have an impact on everything in existence.

3. This train of thought makes me believe that we are all changing the universe in our own special ways. We do this through our mistakes and by finally learning from the mistakes we make. When we change and evolve, it creates a domino effect on our surroundings that, in the long run, will change the world. And when the world is evolving, this will also create changes in the universe.

4. When I consider the great impact our thoughts have, it becomes my goal to be a conscious creator.

5. When you don't understand the power of your own thoughts, you are creating by default. This is how you end up creating things you don't like.

6. By using the soothing technique, you can consciously lift your feelings when you feel low. This also makes life easier for the people around you. This way, you can help make the world a better place for us all.

ASSIGNMENT 1

A. Search for your own soothing words and statements that give you a feeling of relief when you find yourself low on the scale of emotions.

B. See if you can remember situations from the past where you have comforted yourself from negative feelings. What words did you use and what happened to you when you comforted yourself?

I'll start out by doing the assignment and then it will be your turn.

My Turn

If you believe that my emotions are always at the top of the scale, I'm sorry to disappoint you, they're not. Even from one minute to the next, I can slide down to the bottom of the scale. However, I've found this soothing tool picks me up every time.

A. FINDING MY OWN SOOTHING WORDS

Through working in the Foreign Service, moving from one country to the next, I've "lost" many loved ones, not only to death but also by leaving and saying goodbye. I find it very difficult to part from people, places and animals that I've become fond of, and every time I have to say goodbye, I slide down the scale of emotions and fill my mind and heart with sorrow.

The first time I parted with someone I loved dearly was when my first dog died. I was so sad that, when my dad offered me a new dog, I told him I would never want another dog in my whole life.

My dad hugged me and explained that sorrow is a small price to pay for the feeling of love. If I were afraid of the feeling of sorrow, I would choose not to love again because everything will come to an end at some stage.

As you can see from the next picture, I did choose to love a dog again. Since then, I've shared my life with many people, places and animals; and when the day comes that we have to part, I try to remind myself of my father's words: "Sorrow is a small price for love." It always takes me some time to get happy again though, and when the feeling of sorrow and sadness is at its worst, I tell myself, "These emotions will finally also pass."

When things are blocking my path in some way or another, I say to myself, "Maybe I'm putting my focus on the wrong spot on my path," or "There's always a way around an obstacle," or "I don't need to dwell here; I'd rather look for a happy place." Other times, when I'm really unfortunate, instead of becoming angry, I think, "If I survive this, it will become a good story." **Being angry, however, is much better than being depressed and is often required for us to get back on our feet again if something knocks us down.**

HOW I GOT OUT OF DEPRESSION

Going from depression and fear to joy, knowledge, inner strength, freedom, love and gratitude took me a long time. If fear and depression are where you are on the scale of emotions, I believe you can get to the top of the scale much more quickly than I did by using this tool.

Why did it take me so long? I didn't know about the scale of emotions, and I didn't know how to consciously soothe myself to climb to the next step of the scale. Because of this, I took much longer on each step than I needed to. I was also unaware of the need for imbalance to be able to move forward, so I kept on punishing myself for being weak and useless, which just made the situation worse, as self-punishment is the opposite of self-soothing.

B. REMEMBERING PAST SITUATIONS WHEN I'VE COMFORTED MYSELF

When I became ill, my first reaction was to feel sorry for myself, and I slid down into depression. At this stage, I did not know how to comfort myself. As a result of this, my healing processes lasted more than ten years.

After I spent quite some time lying in my bed, life somehow started to move me slowly up the scale and I felt uncertain about my future; then, I felt envious of everybody around me living normal lives. After a while, I became angry with myself for not being able to hold down a job and keep healthy.

From there, I felt discouraged and concerned about my future. I started to have doubts about being able to keep a full-time job again, and I became disappointed with life. Trying to get back to work, I felt overwhelmed, frustrated and impatient over how long it would take me to regain my health, and I started to get really pessimistic about ever being able to have a normal life.

After some years of working a bit on and off, I noticed that my life had become boring and I thought this must be a sign that I could do more with my life; I felt very satisfied with that discovery. From there, I started to feel hope for a brighter future and became optimistic about every positive change in my life. As you can see, I was naturally moving up through the scale.

Since I had to spend so much time in bed, I had plenty of opportunity to read and write. I slowly started to understand that my situation was at least good for something. Now I feel so grateful for the joy and happiness this passion has given me and for all the knowledge I have picked up on my journey from the bottom of the scale of emotions to the top. Finally, I feel free because I now know that the next time I slide down the scale of emotions, I can consciously soothe myself quickly up again, not needing several years for the process!

(I have only answered the parts of the assignments that are relevant for me. Feel free to do the same. However, please read through all the assignment text, because there might be some valuable information hidden there.)

Your Turn

A. First, find where you are on the scale of emotions, then find some soothing words that take you, one step at a time, up the scale so you can feel good.

Keep in mind, however, that if you are going full-speed down an emotional hill and are about to hit the basement floor, there is no point trying to comfort yourself. Your negativity has too much momentum for you to be able to turn your feelings around.

You need to start soothing yourself as soon as you sense that the negative feelings are manifesting themselves in your consciousness. When you're too late, there's nothing you can do other than wait until you hit the ground and then start to "lick your wounds." After a night of good sleep, your feelings will be reset. This is the time to consciously use your mantras and start moving yourself up the scale of emotion again. If you hit the basement once in a while, it doesn't matter. What is important is that you do not allow yourself to be down in the basement more than absolutely necessary.

B. See if you can remember a situation where you comforted yourself up the scale of emotion.

C. Then choose three of your favourite statements and use them as a mantra as soon as you know that your energy and feelings are falling. For each assignment, I will provide suggestions for mantras you can use in addition to your own mantras.

> **MANTRA:** Expansion and growth towards a loving, good and free world is the universal goal.

UPS AND DOWNS

Many faiths interpret our downs as punishment for our sins. I have consciously chosen to believe that humans cannot sin but that we instead make many mistakes. These mistakes give us important experiences that, slowly but surely, lead to growth and expansion for ourselves and ultimately for all mankind.

When life gives us experiences that we don't like, we begin to understand what we really appreciate and start to plan for better living conditions. As we are all created with a longing for expansion and growth, we will not feel happy until we are able to implement our new desires into our lives.

As soon as we launch a desire, our inner being (soul) becomes the expanded version of ourselves. However, if the physical part of us doesn't follow up by listening to the guidance from our inner being, we are separating ourselves from our expanded version and we will feel pain. The worse our feelings become, the more we long for the good feelings. Finally, the bad feelings will force us to move forward so we can experience our own growth. If we do not change, we'll feel so much pain that we'll lose interest in life and eventually die.

However, as far as I believe, death is not meant as a punishment. According to Abraham Hicks, when to leave our body is always an agreement between us and our inner beings. When we do, we trade our bodies for pure consciousness, or for new bodies if we choose to go for another ride. This means that we can never go wrong; our growth just takes longer.

Abraham Hicks also compares life to a trampoline. How high up we jump depends on how far down we go and how conscious our touchdown is.

When I became ill in 2004, I was not very conscious at the moment I started to fall, and I fell on my back instead of my feet. However, after discovering the importance of contrast, I'm now gradually learning how to land on my feet and use the touchdown to reach new highs.

In the next assignment, you will learn how you can turn mistakes into learning and inner growth.

ASSIGNMENT 2

Write a paragraph or two in your journal about how you have previously dealt with pain and your own ups and downs in life.

My Turn

When I had my total breakdown, I felt very sorry for myself and blamed myself and the people around me for making me ill. It took me an unnecessarily long time to understand that the illness had given me a great opportunity to grow, as it created a strong longing for health and prosperity. As soon as I stopped blaming others and myself and instead began to search for happy feelings, my recovery process started.

Your Turn

At this stage, I just want you to become aware of your own falls in life. Write only a few paragraphs, as we shouldn't dwell too long on the past. However, there might be some interesting discoveries here, as I'm quite sure you'll see that your bad experiences have given you the opportunity to grow.

Remember: to make this world a better place, we need change and expansion, so don't beat yourself up for getting out of balance. Imbalance is there for you to make new choices in your life and move yourself forward.

> **MANTRA:** I can learn from my mistakes and lift myself to a new level.

BALANCE AND IMBALANCE

Life is not all about work, exercise or whatever it is that we focus on. To be happy and satisfied, we also need to become conscious about some of the other areas that can make our lives whole and fulfilling, such as spirituality, health, family, personal development, social life, and finances. We have also just discovered that too much happiness and satisfaction will hinder change. Expansion is needed, as that is the nature of life and the purpose of the universe.

Walking or running is a good example for understanding how both balance and imbalance are needed to move forward. We lift one leg up, get imbalanced, put it down again and create new balance; that's how we move forward. If finding balance was our main goal in life, we would not take another step forward, and this would keep us from creating change and expansion. As a result, we would still be living in caves.

ASSIGNMENT 3

A. In your journal, write down some examples of where you have created change and moved forward as a result of losing balance and finding it again.

B. Now find areas in your life where you'd like to find new balance.

My Turn

A. CREATING CHANGE AND MOVING FORWARD

I don't know where to start. My life has been a bumpy road full of falling and learning, and it still is. However, I've now started to accept that this is how we all move forward. By falling, I learned to walk. Being so young, however, I didn't get upset when I lost my balance; babies must know that falling is a natural process of learning.

Nevertheless, when I grew older, I felt really bad when I discovered that my fellow students were much faster learners than I was. Reading and writing are fundamentals to most subjects in school. Taking three years to learn to read and a lifetime to learn how to spell were great setbacks for me. Today I believe my early learning difficulties made me even more determined to learn as an adult. There's nothing I like better than learning through reading and writing, and I'm extremely grateful for this passion.

B. WHERE I NEED TO FIND NEW BALANCE

I need to find new balance in the way I live, to create a better base for a social life. I'm starting to find it too hectic to move around the way I do, living in three different countries during a year. It'll be OK for a few more years, but then I need to settle down. The way I've chosen to live my life means I've become a modern nomad. To choose one country over another might not be easy, but I've really started to feel the need to grow some roots so I can focus more on my social life. This year I will choose to think it through and try to find the best solution.

Your Turn

A. Find some examples in your own life where you have lost your balance then retrieved it and, as a result, moved your life forward.

B. Also find something you would like to work on that you believe needs new balance. Remember to keep the focus on what you want to achieve and not on what you dislike. In other words, focus on the solution and not the problem.

> **MANTRA:** Both balance and imbalance are necessary in order for me to move to new heights.

—That's it for now.

NEXT TIME:

- Discover your dream
- Who are you?
- What are your strengths and weaknesses?

SECOND JOURNEY TOGETHER

DISCOVERING YOUR DREAM

Before coming into this physical experience that we call life, I believe that we each have a vision of what we will make of it. I really struggle to accept that our lives are built on chance. The universe is too complex and wonderful for there to be just coincidence behind our existence. What makes sense to me is that we consciously chose our look, sex, family, country, health and social status in the non-physical realm to help us achieve the goals we made for this lifetime.

Before taking on a new body, I also believe we knew what kinds of activities would make our souls soar. The problem is that, when making big choices for our futures, most of us forget to listen to our own feelings and emotions, which are provided as our guidance system. Therefore, this month, we will spend some time getting to know ourselves better.

If you don't know who you are, what you are good at and what you dream about, it's difficult to take control over your life and to reach where you and your inner being want to go.

ASSIGNMENT 4

Go back to your childhood and write down what you dreamed of doing as an adult.

Most children know what will make them eager and excited. Going back to these memories of who we are and what makes us tick will be very helpful in the search for our dream lives. If you don't remember, no worries. We'll find another way a bit further into our journey.

Another reason for asking you to revisit your childhood is that this was a time when most of us still believed in ourselves. As you pursue your dreams, it will be useful to find out more about what inspired you and filled you with joy before you lost faith in your inner power. If you already know what you dream about, it may still be interesting to do this assignment. You'll then get the opportunity to compare and notice your own development. Besides, you'll see if your dream matches the type of activity you liked when you were young.

As a child, you can dream of many things that you will later discover you do not have enough courage, or the faith in yourself, to accomplish. But you will often see that what you dreamed of as a child will be similar to the fields of interest you have today. What is important to remember, however, is that we all need a dream. Without dreams, it's not easy to change or improve ourselves, and life will soon feel empty, sad and meaningless.

Nevertheless, the dream does not need to be huge at the beginning, only big enough for you to have something to reach for so that you can feel inner growth. Once you see that you are able to create the things you focus on, you will start to believe in yourself, and then you can aim for the stars.

My Turn

What I Dreamed of Doing as an Adult

In 1975, a fourteen-year-old me wrote an essay at school about my dream life. I wanted to write, travel the world and live in Africa.

I was a good storyteller, but my Norwegian teacher told me that it would be difficult for me to become a writer, as I have a form of dyslexia. I thought my teacher might be right because I really struggled to learn how to read, and spelling had never been my thing. In the 1970s we had no computers with spellcheck, and neither my teacher nor I had thought of editors, so I sadly shelved my big dream and went for the second-best option, which was to become a farmer.

I soon discovered that, without hereditary entitlement to a farm, becoming a farmer could be quite tricky, so I shelved that dream too, and went for the third dream: to become a teacher. A teacher who is unable to spell correctly might not be considered a good teacher, and I wanted to be good at my job, so I shelved that dream as well. Nursing was my fourth dream job, but every girl I knew dreamed of becoming a nurse and I didn't want to be like everybody else.

When the time came and I had to choose my studies, I went for business administration, which I did not find very interesting. But at least through this course it would be easy to land a job and earn a decent income, I thought.

Your Turn

You might have dreamed of becoming an astronaut, a firefighter, a singer, a nurse, a scientist, a shop owner ... The dream you once had might be something that today you would not even consider. (Children are often limited in their aspirations simply because they don't know what jobs are out there, or the jobs they will later aspire to may not yet exist).

Do the assignment anyway, as knowing what you dreamed of before life conditioned you and made you unsure about yourself will give you an understanding of what types of activities really excite you and make you happy.

If you don't remember what you dreamed of becoming, you might remember what kind of activities you enjoyed. If so, write down in your journal your favourite hobby as a child and pair it with a job that includes a similar type of activity. Think about if your hobby was based on routines, action, creativity or being on your own, or if it was people-oriented.

> **MANTRA:** With specific dreams and goals for life, I am on my way to taking control of my life.

STRENGTHS AND WEAKNESSES

Understanding who you are and what you are good at, as well as knowing what your weaknesses are, makes it much easier for you to make the right choices in your life. By not knowing who you are, you may punish yourself for not being good enough. This can make the situation worse. You will also lose the opportunity to find your happy path.

My experience is that there's not only one right path but several that eventually lead to the path that makes our souls soar. However, most people stop their growth long before reaching the path at its peak. The reason is that we often misunderstand and think that we all need to fit into the same square box, which is not easy when we might have a different form.

Thinking you have to fit into the same form as your friends, family or society in general can ruin your chance of making the most of your life. If you don't believe in yourself, who will then believe in you? If you permit other people, who don't believe in themselves, to rule you based on their narrow perception of what is right or wrong, or what is possible and impossible, it will be difficult to reach your dreams. If you listen to those who don't have faith in you, this will often cause your dreams to be broken. However, it is never too late to create new dreams.

By doing the next assignment, you can get to know yourself and become proud of who you are, as we all have both strengths and weaknesses and one personality does not need to be better or worse than the other.

ASSIGNMENT 5

Now do the two personality tests below to gain more knowledge about yourself. If you have found your path in life, you can skip the tests; however, you might find them useful to get to know yourself better.

Test Number One:
Identify the three (out of twelve) archetypes you belong to out of the examples below. When you have chosen them, spend some time reflecting on the specific challenges for each archetype. If you find it difficult to choose the archetypes that fit you from the examples below, you can take an archetype test on the Internet to become conscious about your challenges. (You can either take the archetype test using the link at the back of the book or you can google it.)

1.The Athlete
The Athlete is **driven by physical activities**. They thrive on everything related to health, exercise and body, and they really enjoy competition, sports and outdoor activities.

The Athlete's **focus is endurance.**

2. The Rebel

The Rebel is **driven by freedom.** They thrive on wild and uncensored behaviour.

The Rebel's **focus is justice.**

3. The Caregiver

The Caregiver is **driven by relationships**. They thrive on caring and nurturing. Caregivers enjoy the role of parent, sibling, teacher, rescuer, homemaker, best friend or companion.

The Caregiver's **focus is compassion.**

4. The Royal

The Royal is **driven by power.** They thrive on control, entitlement and luxury. Royals enjoy being an executive, CEO, leader, or heir/heiress.

The Royal's **focus is power.**

5. Performer

The Performer is **driven by attention.** They thrive on entertaining and eccentricity. Performers enjoy the role of entertainer, actor and headliner.

The Performer's **focus is electricity.**

6. The Tastemaker

The Tastemaker is **driven by aesthetic.** They thrive on trends, decor and fashion. Tastemakers enjoy the role of host, stylist, goddess, diva and fashion guru.

The Tastemaker's **focus is influence.**

7. The Explorer
The Explorer is **driven by discovery.** They thrive on travel and adventure.

The Explorer's **focus is curiosity.**

8. The Advocate
The Advocate is **driven by cause.** They thrive on social and environmental responsibility. Advocates enjoy the role of defender and champion of a cause.

The Advocate's **focus is hope.**

9. The Intellectual
The Intellectual is **driven by data.** They thrive on thinking and learning. Intellectuals enjoy the role of professional, student, scholar and judge.

The Intellectual's **focus is wisdom.**

10. The Spiritual
The Spiritual is **driven by belief.** They thrive on prayer/meditation and seeking. Spirituals enjoy the role of mystic, healer and seeker.

The Spiritual's **focus is humility.**

11. Visionary
The Visionary is **driven by an idea.** They thrive on hyper-focus and intuition. Visionaries enjoy the role of entrepreneur, innovator, pioneer, guide, or dreamer.

The Visionary's **focus is courage.**

12. The Creative

Creatives are **driven by artistic pursuit**. They thrive on originality, romance and expressing themself through the five senses. Creatives enjoy to perform, create or/and telling stories.

The Creative's **focus is originality**.

My Results

1. Spiritual

2. Visionary

3. Creative

I guess I've grown up to become a spiritual visionary with a hint of creativity. As far as I can remember, I've felt a very strong connection with a higher power, so to be able to connect with this power and discover the meaning and purpose of life has therefore become essential to me. I have discovered that it makes me very happy and content when I spend time on spiritual stuff. In the past, if I haven't created time for meditation, conscious living and spiritual reflections, I have become sick.

I'm also an entrepreneur, a guide and a dreamer, making me a visionary person. I love to find new and better ways of living to make myself and others thrive. I'm also creative. I write, I paint and I love interesting designs. However, I believe I'm first and foremost spiritual and visionary. My creativity, however, is helpful in my quest to share my thoughts about conscious living with the world.

From the test, I understand that my challenge is to remain committed to my vision in order to bring it to fruition, and I need to develop my talent and express myself without letting fear of failure and criticism hold me back.

I think I became spiritual through my childhood family frequently asking the big questions: "Why am I here?" "What's my purpose in life?" "What happens after death?"

During my childhood, my family and I visited several organised religions, seeking answers to our questions. Not finding a more convincing answer elsewhere, my parents kept their Christian Sunday School beliefs. They seldom visit our church, but they find peace in meditation and prayers.

As for me, I believe my upbringing made me think outside the box. I didn't find satisfying answers to my big questions inside any organised religion; thoughts about sin, shame and punishment were not compatible with my strong desire to feel good. I've also checked out Buddhism and Hinduism, but lately I have discovered that I feel great just by following my inner spirit. The spirit within does not dictate or use dogmas to steer me in any direction. This way I feel free. And being free is my ultimate goal for this lifetime.

Test Number Two

The personality test I have used is called 16 Personalities. (See the link at the back of the book.) However, feel free to use one of your own choosing. What is important is that you get to know yourself better.

You belong to one of sixteen different personality types, divided into four groups. Under the group categories of Analyst, Diplomat, Sentinel and Explorer, you will find four subgroups that explain who you are.

My Turn

Below you can see the result of my test.

ENFP Personality (The campaigner)
90% EXTROVERT

Diplomat
80% INTUITIVE

Folk mastery
50% FEELINGS

I find my test result quite accurate and helpful, and everything I'm doing falls into the above categories. Having this knowledge, I know I'm doing the things that are in my lane and that the platform I'm now standing on is the base from which I can make my leap.

I also find it important to know my weaker sides; with this knowledge, I can choose tasks that challenge me by training myself to become the person I'd really like to be.

Through this test, I have understood that I love to initiate new ideas, but I do not find it fun to do too much routine work. This is very true. I am also very sensitive to criticism. These are two examples of weaknesses of my kind of personality. Using this insight, I can easily challenge myself, or I can do the opposite and make sure that I mainly do things that I'm good at. For example, I have chosen to expose myself to criticism by writing this guide.

The routine work of maintaining my website, on the other hand, I have chosen to give to others who like this kind of work. As you can see, we will not be equally interested in challenging all our weaknesses. And that's fine too, as long as we make these choices consciously.

Your Turn

Please study your results in detail, getting to know both your strengths and your weaknesses, as this knowledge can come in handy when you make big decisions in your life.

Remember that none of these test results are set in stone. Everything in the world is changing and we are changing with it, which is supposed to be good news. The challenge is that most of us don't like change. Long before this journey is over, though, you'll hopefully learn to appreciate change and start yearning for growth.

* Should you feel that these two tests don't describe you, take the tests again and try to answer the questions honestly. Should you still not agree, describe your personality in your journal/workbook. Find six strong qualities and six weak qualities in yourself. The weak qualities are the ones you have the potential to improve. The strong qualities are the areas you know that you have already mastered and can build on.

How far are you from reaching your dream?

Knowing how far you are from reaching your dream does not tell you anything about how long it will take you to reach your destination. However, if you see that you are living at odds with your dream, this discovery will hopefully encourage you to make changes in your life. The time it takes to reach your dream depends only on how determined you are to change and how willing you are to get into the mood to receive the good stuff in life.

ASSIGNMENT 6

A. With the knowledge you now have about yourself, find out how much you are living according to your dream and to your personality, and give both a number between 1 and 10, with 1 as the "furthest from" score.

B. Maybe you need a new direction for your life. If so, start to think about where you want to go. You might not need to change your path, but rather find tasks on your path that are more in your lane.

My Turn

A. Living My Dream

At the moment, if I'm not a 10, I'm at least very close to living my childhood dream – score 9.9 – which means my life has started to yearn for new challenges and new growth.

Comparing my personality to the kind of work I do, I'm also very close: score 9. To be able to give it a 10, I would need to work together with likeminded people, as I really want more outlets for my extroverted side.

My life has changed tremendously since I first started my inner journey towards conscious living. After doing this assignment, I realised that I've done all that I had on my list as a child. I've travelled around the world, I'm a writer, I've lived in many countries in Africa – Tanzania, The Gambia, Uganda, South-Sudan, South Africa – and I'm currently living in Ethiopia.

In Banjul, The Gambia, I had a mini "farm" with goats, chickens and ducks and a beautiful fruit and vegetable garden. In Juba, South-Sudan, I taught traumatised children how to read. In Kampala, Uganda, I built a school for street children. In Dar es Salaam, Tanzania, I saved several lives just through teaching the importance of giving enough fluid to babies with diarrhoea and vomiting. And in Norway, I nursed at a home for people with disabilities while studying.

B. New Direction for My Life

However, it's through *this* journey that I'm now living my dream. Doing the personality test again after a few years, I can see how I have strengthened my personality as I've become much more intuitive, assertive and spiritual, and instead of being as adventurous as before, I've become more vision-ary. Going on this journey myself, I'm able to do what I enjoy the most at this stage of my life. I just love the feeling of inner growth, and the reason why I enjoy writing about it so much is that it really echoes my personality.

Your Turn

If you discover that you are not living a life according to your personality, you can study the results to get a better understanding of who you are: your strengths and also your weaknesses. Combining this with looking into what kind of activities you dreamed of doing as a child might give you a clue as to where you can take your life to feel happier and more excited about yourself.

Looking at the career advice for your personality type, you can find out what you can change in terms of studies, work or hobbies to be able to get yourself on the happy track. However, this doesn't mean that you need to change your path. With this information, you can discover where to put your focus on the path you are on. For instance, if you are an adventur-ous or creative person, and your job or studies don't give much outlet for this passion, you can find a hobby that does.

If you find that you are living according to your personality and your child-hood dream but still don't feel satisfied about your life, there are plenty of life-changing discoveries to be made on this journey. It can be useful, though, to study the results and get to know yourself better; maybe you'll discover new things about yourself that you were not aware of.

I hope you see the value of becoming better acquainted with yourself.

Now you can be proud of your personality and discover the value of the qualities and the strengths you actually have. I hope that this knowledge will also make it easier for you to have faith in yourself and your dream.

Should you have forgotten what you dreamed of when you were younger or should you see that you have fulfilled your big dream, a better insight into who you are and why you are here will hopefully inspire you to create new dreams.

> **MANTRA:** If I do not have a dream, I can still find something to dream about.

—That's it for now.

NEXT TIME:

- How happy thoughts bring happy situations
- The magic in feeling grateful
- How to fill our days with happiness

THIRD JOURNEY
TOGETHER

CONSCIOUS THOUGHTS

There are two theories out there for how happy thoughts bring happy situations or how crappy thoughts bring crappy situations. Choose the one you feel is most convincing to you. The important thing is that you understand that your thoughts and feelings matter, so you'll make an effort to choose your thoughts consciously.

Theory 1. Physical Thoughts
Theory 2. The Law of Attraction

PHYSICAL THOUGHTS

Tim Bronson points out in his blog that neuroscientists have now discovered that a thought is a physical pathway in the brain. The more you think the same thought, the more you groove and strengthen the path and make it easier to have the same thought again and again. That's why having the thought "I never get it right" or "life sucks" is not a great idea, as you start to create a self-fulfilling prophecy.

The brain hates holding two contradictory opinions at once because it creates cognitive dissonance, so when you tell yourself "life sucks," your brain seeks out information to back up what you are saying and overlooks everything that contradicts it.

THE LAW OF ATTRACTION

Since Rhonda Byrne launched her book *The Secret,* many people have started to accept the concept of "We create our life through the way we think and feel." However, this knowledge is very old and goes way back to the first thinkers on our planet.

Chanakya, Indian politician and writer (350–275 BC) said, "Your feelings are your god." (God = creator.) The Greek philosopher Epictetus (AD 55–135) said, "It's not what happens to you, but how you react to it that matters."

I find Abraham Hicks' explanation of why our feelings have such great power especially fascinating: everything in the universe is made of energy. Energy is always moving and changing and can take the form of all things we are able to imagine. We just need to imagine it first.

This implies that everything we create starts with a thought. If you have chosen to believe in the Bible, this was the way God created the Earth, and if you believe we are God's children made in his image, it makes sense that we, too, are creators and create through our thoughts and words.

However, if we are not conscious of what we think about, we can create a lot of stuff and situations we don't want, such as described in the Bible story when God became angry with his unconscious children and created the flood, regretting it afterwards and promising he would never make this mistake again.

I look at the story of Noah as a parable that shows that we learn through our mistakes. Even such a big mistake, like drowning almost the entire population of the world, does not play a particularly important role from an eternal perspective.

Nicola Tesla (1856–1943), the inventor of the radio and alternating current, said, "If you want to find the secret of the universe, think in terms of energy, frequency and vibration."

SO, LET'S TRY IT OUT:

Rhonda Byrne asks us to think of our thoughts as energy that vibrates at different frequencies, like a radio. We can choose which frequency we want to receive by choosing our thought. If our thoughts and feelings are vibrating at a high frequency, we will receive what is broadcast at that frequency. If our thoughts and feelings are vibrating at a low frequency, we receive what is broadcast by this "station."

In other words, when you meet someone who is angry or happy, you can feel their vibrations even if they don't say a word. If a person feels happy, you will usually also feel happy in meeting this person. If the person feels irritated or angry and you are not conscious, there is a high probability that you will pick up this low frequency and react in an annoyed or angry way, even before the person speaks. If we add words to the experience, the bad feelings will be further reinforced.

This is why, when you think fearful thoughts, you are more prone to experience the fearful situations found on the low-frequency station.

If you are not able to change your thoughts and feelings, you'll soon get into a loop of bad creations. The opposite goes for the good thoughts.

Thoughts trigger emotions, which again attract good and bad situations depending on whether your thoughts are good or bad. The stronger your feelings are, the stronger the consequences of your thoughts become.

The vast majority of people are not conscious of what they think and feel. The reason we are not more critical of what we choose to think is that we do not understand that it is the thought that triggers our feelings and that it is our emotions that subsequently attract the situations in our lives.

When we do not understand the consequences of our own thoughts, we become like a ping-pong ball that only responds to stimuli from outside, and thus we lose control over our lives.

However, if you grasp the importance of deliberately shifting your focus to a positive thought, for example through self-soothing when you feel down, you will avoid negative chain reactions. Then you will be able to steer your life towards good thoughts that will trigger good feelings and, again, attract good situations.

In other words, your thoughts affect your emotions, which in turn affect your actions. The interesting thing is that your thoughts will also be able to influence other people's feelings and actions. The significance of your own thoughts therefore becomes much more important than you first thought.

One of these perspectives may resonate more deeply than the other. Either way, we now know that we create our own lives through the way we think.

ASSIGNMENT 7

In your journal, write down examples of beliefs that have previously made you miserable and how changing those beliefs made you feel happy.

My Turn

Beliefs That Have Previously Made Me Feel Bad

I don't know where to start ... there are so many things I've believed in the past that have made me feel miserable, where choosing to believe differently changed my life. However, I'll pick just one for now as an example and we'll discuss the others later as they fit into our journey.

I've decided to choose beauty as, just the other day, I had to work on my feelings and beliefs again when I was tagged on Facebook with a picture showing me from a very unflattering angle, to put it mildly. I'm laughing now, but when I first saw it, I quickly cancelled the photo from my Facebook page, feeling annoyed that the tagger would post such an awful picture on my behalf.

At my age, letting a Facebook picture make me miserable is below my standards, especially when I'm writing about conscious living, so I had to choose to see the situation differently.

A few hours later, I discovered why this photo made me feel so bad. The Facebook picture came at a bad time. I wasn't in a good mood, as I had just discovered that my favourite dress didn't fit me anymore, and this picture just added to my feeling of annoyance and low self-worth, and I lost balance.

Losing Balance + Finding Balance = Growth

It was not until I had started writing again after my lunch break that I remembered, "It's not what happens to us but how we react that matters." Finally, I stopped being hard on myself and tried the soothing technique instead. Eventually, I was able to laugh at my few extra kilos and see the beauty in getting mature and, I hope, wiser, and I found new balance.

It seems that I might not have learned this lesson fully, though. As far as I know myself, there will be other situations where I need to soothe myself on the same subject in the future. But that's OK, as long as I remember my tools. The situation will only bring potential for more growth.

Beauty is in the eyes of the beholder, they say. However, what others think of me is not important compared to what I think of myself. I guess most people who saw this picture of me would not have even noticed what was so bad about it, and, if they did, they would have thought either "Nina is changing as she's getting older," or, "Oh, my! That was an unfortunate angle for a Facebook picture!" and my unflattering picture would have made them laugh. Anyhow, what they would have thought doesn't matter. What I think about myself, though, can build or ruin my feeling of self-worth and my life.

Most people would like to look beautiful, but to what extent they are willing to work for it differs. If we could accept our bodies as they are, we would definitely make it much easier for ourselves to be happy. We can focus on the parts that are beautiful; if there is no beauty as far as the eye can see, there are usually other beautiful things to focus on, such as a beautiful voice (works marvellously on the radio) or a beautiful personality (which is appreciated everywhere).

At least it's good to know that our friends will not choose us for our beauty, but rather for all the other brilliant things about us. When it comes to finding a lover, our look is often the first impression. However, it's the mix of personality, interests, knowledge, charm, humour and self-worth that will make our relationships last.

Our body will lose its youthful beauty sooner or later. Our inner beauty, on the other hand, has the potential for everlasting growth and is really worth investing in, not only for the sake of making friends and finding a lover, but mainly for us to feel at home and free inside our bodies and live happy, interesting lives.

> If you struggle with extreme obesity, anorexia, bulimia or other eating disorders, it will be especially important to accept yourself just the way you are, as eating disorders often originate from low self-worth.

If we lose respect for our bodies, we will not care enough about giving our bodies the nutrition and activity they need to function optimally. If we start loving ourselves, however, we will be kind to our bodies through our choice of constructive good thoughts. The good thoughts will in turn lead to good feelings, which in turn will lead to good actions and, ultimately, to a healthy, energetic and happy body.

> Abraham says that our bodies do not have to become frail and sick with age. Because we see other old and sick people around us, we believe we will also get sick with age. And when we believe that our vision, hearing or skeleton will weaken as we grow old, it will.

On the other hand, our appearance will always be changing. An infant will look very different after just a few months. A twelve-year-old will look different when he or she is in her twenties. Likewise, a forty-year-old will look very different when he or she turns eighty.

Even so, in spite of age, we can still look and feel healthy and be full of energy until the day we die. Abraham explains that weakness in old age comes only from negative thoughts or an unconscious desire to gradually end life.

I'm afraid I have a way to go before I am this conscious. However, having this knowledge has started to inspire me to change my focus.

Your Turn

How can you change your beliefs about yourself and your life to make it easier to feel happy?

By becoming conscious about what you focus on and what you choose to believe, you can set yourself up for success instead of failure. You are the one who knows what is needed to make yourself feel happy.

If you choose not to be happy before you are perfect in all areas of your life, you are definitely going to fail. When you choose happiness as your highest priority, you just need to feel grateful, and the feeling of happiness will be yours in a fraction of a second.

> **MANTRA:** How I feel is a result of how I choose to think.

GRATEFULNESS

There is no better way of ending your day than by being grateful. Why? Because this is the time that you set your mood for the next day. You might think that you have nothing to be grateful for, but if you are breathing, which I'm sure you are, you can be grateful for being alive.

Abraham Hicks explains it this way: we're all eternal beings going in and out of physical and non-physical existence, but it's in our physical existence that we have the greatest potential for inner growth.

You create your life through the way you think and feel. If you can also manage to be grateful for your obstacles and pain, you'll soon change your unfortunate situation into a fortunate one and you'll become an inspiration for others.

On the other hand, if you can't manage to be grateful, and you focus only on your misfortune, your feelings will slide down to the negative vibrations on the scale of emotions to the station where negativity is broadcast. That means you'll suffer more misfortune.

People who struggle with depression may have great difficulty finding things they are grateful for. By making it a routine to focus each morning and evening on the things, people or situations that you appreciate, this exercise will give you relief from negative thoughts. This presupposes that you will not be disappointed in yourself on the days when you are not able to find something to be grateful for.

ASSIGNMENT 8

Every day, write down in your journal examples of things in your life that you are grateful for. Eventually, you will not need to write gratitude lists, as you will truly feel so grateful for your life that "thank you" will be a mantra that you'll say to yourself every time you're reminded of how good life can be.

My Turn

MY GRATITUDE LIST

The more grateful I've become, the more things and situations I've received to be grateful about. My list is endless, and I guess yours will be too before we finish this journey together.

Below, you'll find a short version of my gratitude list as an example.

I just love my life and everything about it. At least, most of it – there are a few things I'd like to change, and I'm working on it.

I have my ups and downs, and I'm very grateful for the potential this gives me for more growth.

I love my two dogs, who bestow me with unconditional love. I'm really so, so grateful.

I love my body, my legs and arms, and all my senses, which make me feel free and independent.

I love my ability to enjoy this planet, nature and all the time I spend in it, as this fills me with happiness as soon as I focus my attention on the birds, animals and plants around me.

I'm grateful for my new pillow that is small and soft and fits so well under my head, supporting me when I sleep.

I love my shower and the lovely warm water that rinses my body every morning and wakes me up for a new day.

I love music that hits me in the heart and makes me dance or lifts my mood until I feel I'm floating in tune with the rhythm.

I'm incredibly grateful for books, movies and TV series that make me laugh or that draw me into other people's worlds and situations. They give me excitement, joy and a better insight into my own life.

I'm indescribably grateful for shops, roads, schools, hospitals and airports and all the people needed to make everything work in planning, construction, operation and maintenance. They make my life easier to live.

I'm so grateful for the Internet, my kitchen and bathroom, electricity, my sofa, my clothes and shoes, and for my car, which all make my life so much more practical.

I'm so grateful to be able to sit here on my sofa writing my list of gratuities, while feeling the bliss of gratitude spread throughout my entire body.

I'm so grateful to be alive and to feel that my purpose is to change, grow and be happy. And I'm really, really so grateful when I get a chance to be an uplifter of others so they, too, can enjoy their lives in this eternally expanding universe, and to make life on Earth evolve, one conscious step at a time.

Before you do your assignment, please listen to Nick Vujicic on this book's website. He has no legs or arms, and travels around the world as an inspiring, motivational speaker. His motto is: "No Arms, No Legs, No Worries" (www.a-life-worth-living.org/feel-good-links/inspiration/).

Your Turn

Creating gratitude lists is a very good way to get in touch with your inner being. As soon as you feel joy and love for yourself and the world around you, you will be at the same vibration-frequency as your inner being and you will be able to listen to directions that will lead you to your dream.

When making gratitude lists, it is important to focus on things in your life that don't evoke bad feelings. It is therefore advisable to include items such as your bed, duvet or pillow, nature, laughter and pleasure, flowers, birds and animals. If you have problems with your body, family, friends or job, do not include these in your gratitude list.

Expand your list every evening as you go to bed, and you'll soon tune your "broadcasting station" to the good music that will make your life rock.

> **MANTRA:** When I am grateful, I attract situations, items and people that give me reason to be even more grateful.

HAPPINESS

We're all built in such a way that the further we are from being happy, the more pain we'll experience. Our inner being (which I have chosen to believe is the extension of the Source) disagrees with anything that is not making us happy. As soon as we think negatively about ourselves, others or a situation, our feelings drop because, by thinking negatively, we remove ourselves from our joyful journey and the way the Source sees us.

Abraham Hicks compares our feelings to a cork floating on a river. The cork is happy dancing down the river on its life journey. It is you and me who force it down under water when we start thinking negative thoughts. As soon as we let go of the negative thoughts, the cork pops back to the surface again and continues dancing happily down the river.

Abraham also compares our life to a river in how we struggle through life forcing ourselves to work hard, thinking life is supposed to go upstream.

However, that's not the direction of a good life. By turning around on our backs and floating downstream, we would enjoy life tremendously and go much further on our journey.

If you believe that life is meant to be heavy and stressful, there is a high likelihood that life will feel tiresome. However, if you believe that life is meant to be exciting and challenging, like a kayaker who will experience both calm and challenging stretches on the way down the river, the probability will be greater for life to be exciting, fun and educational.

When life is really difficult, however, it is not easy to understand how it is possible to feel good. If you are completely down in the basement of your emotions, what I write here will just feel annoying. If this is the case, put the book away and try to cheer yourself up by doing something you know will lift your spirits before continuing to read on.

You might ask, "**How can I be happy when I experience so many challenges in life?**" I have chosen to believe that my hunger for inner growth was already strong in the non-physical when I was going to pick a new body. As a result, I chose to enter a body that does not function perfectly. Having parents who asked questions about life gave me the urge to search for answers. And, over time, I have found solutions that have helped me cope with my challenges.

My solutions may not be right for you, but I'm convinced that you will find solutions to your challenges as soon as you are willing to listen inward. You are not alone; no one is alone. We all go through bad times in our lives. But we must endure the night to be able to experience a new day in the same way that we must endure the rain to again experience sunshine.

By selecting a higher peak, we're more likely to have a greater view than somebody choosing to stay at home – assuming we don't break our neck on the way up, of course. Being negative or rushing, striving and beating ourselves up for not moving faster will only drain us of energy. However, knowing that we can do it and that we have the ability to get through the challenges on our way up will give us energy and the likelihood of us reaching the peak of our life will be much higher.

The question is, how can you let go of the cork?
You can stop acting without thinking and continue only when what you do makes you happy. You might ask, "But not everybody can be happy, right? Somebody needs to do the sucky jobs on this planet." The answer is both yes and no. You can be happy doing any job if you don't consider what you do to be sucky.

You might think wiping yourself after going to the toilet is a sucky job, but most people do it without thinking of it this way because it is more satisfying to clean ourselves than not. We even wipe the poop off our babies to make them happy, because making our babies happy makes us happy. Helping our neighbours, friends or family makes them happy, and seeing them happy makes us happy too.

If you think your job is poorly paid, you can still choose to think the job is great for now because you are happier with the security of having some income rather than none. Turning onto your back and enjoying the ride will automatically change the broadcasting station to the one with the good music. By keeping yourself up in the high frequencies with the good music, the chance of your boss giving you a raise or a new job opportunity is also much higher.

However, if you do any of these things with an attitude of "I'm the one doing the sucky jobs, and nobody does anything for me," you lose the opportunity to feel happy and tune instead to a low-frequency station broadcasting more of the bad stuff.

If you think your thoughts don't matter, you'll have to think again. Every thought matters. Nevertheless, there's no need to panic, as getting out of balance is a must for growth and expansion. To be able to move forward though, you need to find a new balance. This is done simply by being conscious of how you think about your life and looking out for every opportunity to feel good.

ABRAHAM'S FIVE STEPS
THE PROCESS OF ATTRACTING YOUR DREAM

First step: you create a wish.
The wish is formed as a result of discomfort. When you experience something you don't like, you begin to understand what you do like, and a new wish is being visualised.

Second step: the wish manifests itself in the non-physical/ in your inner being.
The wish manifests itself the moment you have visualised it. However, it can't be part of your physical life until you are a vibrational match to your wish.

Third step: you manage to feel what it's like to live out your dream without the dream having manifested itself in your life yet.
You become a vibrational match to the dream by raising your feelings through gratitude, soothing, meditation, having fun, etc.

Fourth step: you manage to keep yourself in the high vibrations of good emotions for a long time.

This is done by starting each day consciously and by trying as best as possible to keep yourself up in the high vibrations as the day proceeds.

Fifth step: you forgive yourself for not being able to be conscious all the time and keep your feelings high.

This you do by soothing yourself out of the low vibrations before you attract too many negative consequences.

The question will now be: How can I manage to flow happily down the river more often so that I can stay longer in the high vibrations?

This can be done by learning what makes you happy and filling your life with more of those things.

ASSIGNMENT 9

A. First, think about how to look at your life differently to make your cork float. Which stories will you leave out, and which will you keep or change so you can feel more positive about your situation?

B. In your journal, write down examples of things that make you happy, preferably things that don't cost money, and start to include these activities in your daily life.

My Turn

A. How to Look at Life Differently

When I was ill, I was so focused on my own problems that I used every opportunity to talk about my misfortune when meeting family and friends.

It wasn't until I stopped this habit that I was able to create a new and better life for myself.

B. List of the Things That Make Me Happy

- reading good books
- philosophising over life
- watching people on the street
- watching the stars
- smelling herbs and flowers
- making plans
- watching the clouds
- listening to birds and insects
- taking a bath
- cuddling
- giving and receiving massages
- giving advice
- making others laugh and smile
- telling stories
- being childish
- making funny faces
- being kind
- swimming
- playing tennis
- yoga
- meditation
- being with friends and family
- watching good movies
- writing screenplays
- short stories and novels
- teaching
- painting and drawing
- sculpting
- dancing
- playing with my animals
- cooking a meal together with family and friends
- giving someone a helping hand
- calling my family
- listening to music
- singing and whistling
- watching the sunrise and sunset
- gardening

- hiking
- giving compliments and seeing other people's strength
- talking with strangers
- being in nature
- listening to Abraham Hicks
- rowing in the fjords of Norway
- kayaking and snorkelling in Tanzania
- playing in the sand on the beach
- growing my own herbs and vegetables
- horse riding
- being on my brother's farm
- playing with children
- holding and smelling babies
- touching soft things
- dressing up in my nice or silly outfits
- looking at family photos
- decorating my home
- reading palms and faces
- sleeping
- taking a nap
- imitating the sounds of birds
- picking berries in the woods
- watching wildlife
- smiling
- laughing at my own jokes
- playing cards and games
- taking photos
- learning new skills
- meeting new people and experiencing new cultures

Your Turn

A. Choose only happy stories to tell about yourself and try to leave the sad stories behind. It's no use reminding yourself about them all the time, because it only keeps them alive. If there's only one good thing to tell about yourself, put your emphasis there and keep quiet about the other stuff until you are able to feel differently about it. In other words, if you have big problems, keep your focus on the solutions.

The vast majority of us will not be able to do this in the first phase of a difficult situation. But as your energy increases and you begin to get the painful situation at a distance, your awareness will increase and you will be able to more easily choose what you want to focus on.

If you have major problems, contact someone who you know wishes you well. Ask them to help you find solutions while reminding you of everything that works in your life. If you manage to feel grateful for what is actually working well, good solutions for what isn't working will be easier to discover.

B. Make a list of at least fifty things that make you happy. Every day, do three things that make you feel good. Rotate them according to your mood and situation, and have fun with it.

> **MANTRA:** As I make my bed, so I must lie on it.

Before we end this session ... What makes me happy might be totally different from what makes you happy, as we might have opposite personalities, and that's one of the things that makes life so interesting.

Remember the scale of emotions? Sometimes we are angry, frustrated, sad and disappointed, and that's OK too. So don't beat yourself up when your mood drops. The feelings are there only because you don't see yourself, others or a situation in the right light. Soothing is the way, not criticising yourself or others.

Also remember to take it slowly, one emotion at a time, and you'll soon be at the top of the scale of emotions. Then you might drop again – that's how we grow. The topography of our life journey is not flat. Our life journey goes up, down and sideways, and sometimes we even need to backtrack to find a new route.

The journey can be exciting at times, while other times it's tough and painful, but I can promise you it's rewarding when you are able to see the view from the top, feeling proud that you made it. You made it to the top of this peak, but don't worry, there'll be more peaks to come – more fun, more excitement, some more pain and, finally, more growth. And on and on it goes.

The more conscious we become though, the less painful our journeys will be. Anyway, some pain will be necessary, as all growth feels challenging. To suffer, on the other hand, is a choice we can deselect.

> Some examples of growing pain: when we grow up as a child, when we exercise and build muscles, when we climb a mountain or when we try to change and evolve.

You might find it exhausting, this eternity of growth. Luckily, most of us forget our previous lives and get a totally fresh start when we are born. However, this is not always the case. On my website, you can watch a video about a little boy who remembers his past life. **www.a-life-worth-living.org** Look under feel good/inspiration.

—That's it for now.

NEXT TIME:

- Why do we have different religions?

- Learning how to meditate

- How to make the right decisions

FOURTH JOURNEY
TOGETHER

RELIGION

Since I was very young, I've been asking myself why there are so many religions. The answers I have found might not be "the truth, the whole truth and nothing but the truth so help me God," but they give me a deeper understanding of why we humans have such different views of God, our origin and why we are here.

Before I decided, at the age of fifteen, that I wanted to be confirmed, I read the Bible. I found the messages very disturbing, especially the parts in the Old Testament about Hell and revenge, although I found the love and forgiveness parts of the New Testament nice and soothing. But I couldn't make sense of these messages, as they totally contradicted each other. I therefore decided to focus only on the New Testament.

Later in my life, as I compared different religions, I discovered that most religions are grounded on the same few messages: love, peace and eternal life, and different laws on how to fulfil the requirements for reaching the eternal place of peace and love.

Based on the above findings, I began to look at the differences between religions in the same way as I look at the differences between cultures. The religion and culture of a region reflect each other, and sometimes it is difficult to distinguish between the two.

As far as I can see, many religions have something good to offer but also bad, as most religions are more or less based on fear. The more fearful one religion is, the less the focus is on love and peace, and the greater the distance is between God and man.

The religion or culture you belong to will not prevent you from achieving your dream, as long as you remain autonomous and free. Having something greater than yourself to believe in may be useful, as your faith can comfort you and keep you going despite the dark periods of your life. In other words, what language we use to describe our spiritual experience does not matter, as far as I can see.

Many people do not get comfort from religion though, which may be due to the fact that several religions have a dark history. The main goal of the religious leaders might not have been to soothe the believers, but rather to control them through fear, extracting money from the congregation and, not least, robbing them of belief in their own inner power.

Religions have also been the cause of countless mass killings. As you have probably observed, these exploitations do not belong to the past, as even today abuse is exercised in the name of God.

In order to make a conscious choice about what you believe, you can use your feelings to lead you towards a belief that resonates with your inner being. The purpose of religion or belief is, in my opinion, to help us feel peace, security and love, and not the opposite: turmoil, fear and hatred.

As I said before, the reason I am writing about religion in this guide is not that I want you to change your religion, but rather to inspire you to become aware of what you want to focus on in the religious community you already belong to.

Should you, on the other hand, not believe in anything greater than yourself, my desire is to encourage you to at least gain faith in yourself and your inner power.

Having spent a large part of my life as a "nomad," living in many different cultures and experiencing many different religions, I have learned to appreciate aspects from several religious communities. As a consequence, I have deliberately chosen to practise the parts I find useful in my daily quest for peace and love here on Earth. My focus is first and foremost here in this life, and not so much in the non-physical or "Paradise," as some prefer to call it. I do not think I'll end up in an everlasting peaceful paradise, as such a thought does not appeal to me.

If everything was perfect, what would we do – just sit there and smile at each other? An eternal life in a perfect paradise is a thought that feels unbearably boring to me.

I have probably experienced too many years of unproductive life while I was sick to be able to comfort myself with such a thought. What I like, however, is inner growth and learning, and I love the idea of an ever-expanding universe. I believe that when I've finished all my discoveries on Earth, I will choose new adventures somewhere else.

These thoughts may not appeal to you. You may look forward to rest in a peaceful, happy paradise, and I do not intend to take away this belief. Instead, I think that one theory does not have to exclude the other, as we see that in life we also have different preferences. Some people prefer to stay at home, while others enjoy being on the move.

The reason we have so many different religions, I think, lies precisely in our different needs for comfort. On the other hand, there are obviously few people who choose their religion consciously. Instead, our religion is often presented to us by our parents and the society we grow up in long before we are able to make our own choices.

It is also interesting to note that very few religious communities regard man as an extension of the non-physical Source energy.

Nor are there many religious communities that have given man the responsibility for the creation of expansion and change towards an ever better, freer and more loving world.

Even fewer religions preach that our world's expansion is through human trials, error and, eventually, learning. Instead, in the vast majority of faith communities, our mistakes are perceived as sin.

And why is that? Without fear, shame and sin, religion would not function as a method of control. The question is whether we want our belief to be something that other people will use to control us or if we want our faith to give us comfort, love and strength to enable us to steer our lives in the direction we want to go.

In any case, it should be up to you to choose what resonates with your inner being so you can feel peace, love and happiness. What makes you happy might not be what makes me happy. To be able to respect that we are different and appreciate that we do not need to have the same beliefs might be the first step in the direction of love and peace on Earth.

ASSIGNMENT 10

A. If you belong to a religion and feel uneasy, first think through which parts of your religion make you feel happy. Then think through which parts of your religion make you feel sad.

B. In your journal, write down what beliefs you'll focus on to help you to reach the top of the scale of emotions. It's important to consciously question what you want to believe in, because your belief is so powerful that it can make you happy or sad, weak or strong, loving or hateful.

By being conscious and not just following the crowd, you take responsibility for your own life. This advice also goes for what I'm writing here. If what I believe doesn't resonate with your inner being, choose to believe differently, but make sure that what you choose to believe makes you feel good.

My Turn

Thoughts around My Religion

I was born on Easter morning on a beautiful sunny Sunday. My mum used to sing a Norwegian hymn to me every Easter, which goes something like this: "Easter morning extinguish sorrow, extinguish sorrow forever and ever ..."

Then she would say, "Happy birthday, my sweet little angel – you made my life worth living."

Growing up with a mother who really loved me and who put emphasis on me being born on the same day that the Christian world celebrates Jesus' resurrection might have had something to do with my interest in Jesus.

Nevertheless, I was not able – and I promise you that I tried – to see Jesus as the son of God more than I or other people are. The only difference I can see is that Jesus had a much stronger connection with the Source. Being connected to the Source and his inner being, Jesus was a great teacher with an extraordinarily strong feeling of love and an extraordinary knowledge about how we all can make this connection.

I've always interpreted Jesus' pain on the cross as everybody's pain and as a catalyst for a better and more loving future. It's not only Jesus who felt pain for the sake of our growth; we all do. The understanding of why we need to feel pain will, however, give us courage to face the pain over and over again, just as a woman might choose to go through painful childbirth again and again for the sake of receiving a new life.

As our insight increases, however, we learn how to live and also give birth to children without excessive pain, and the world will move towards becoming a better and less painful place.

B. My Religious Focus

Jesus is my idol, and I really love the way he taught through parables. I also love him for being such a great role model for us all. To become as good as him, to keep myself up at the top of the scale of emotions, is a great goal. Whether this is possible, however, I really don't know, but I have chosen to believe that Jesus was a human being just like we all are. Jesus, on the other hand, had the ability to stay on top of the emotion scale, more often than all of us, but not even he was able to live a life completely without pain.

We all need to feel pain to move this world forward. Our pain and low vibrations are, on the other hand, an indication that we are moving in the wrong direction of our dream. In fact, we should embrace our negative feelings, as they are our only guiding tools.

However, we don't need to be in the low vibrations for a long time, only long enough to change our focus towards what we now desire from life. And what we want is usually to return to our happy paths to continue our journeys. Nevertheless, some people choose to end this journey as a result of their challenges, but their mission on Earth might now be complete.

A few years ago, I made a drawing of Jesus to remind myself of his extraordinary knowledge and love. Later, I regretted that I didn't draw him smiling. It's his teaching about love and his promise of a better future that I want to focus on, not so much the suffering that he went through.

(I recommend you watch the movie *Breathe,* as this movie might open your eyes to how your challenges can become a great gift to our world.)

Your Turn

You may have a different view of religion than I do, and yet there might be things in your religion that disturb you and make you unable to feel good.

An example may be if your religion does not accept your sexual preference. Not being accepted for who you are can be very depressing. This is why many people with non-heterosexual dispositions have committed suicide, as they think that their creator does not accept them either.

If you belong to a religion that stigmatises your sexual preference, you can choose to think differently and focus only on those parts of your religion that make you happy, rejecting the other parts.

Most holy writings were written by learned men for people who couldn't read or write themselves. These people lived long before our time and therefore had a completely different view of life and humankind than we have today.

The Scriptures also tell about events that took place long before they were written down, which gives great room for misinformation. Moreover, the events were often written as parables and are therefore open to interpretation. Some claim, nevertheless, that the written word is holy and must be interpreted literally. The challenge is that even the written word can be perceived differently.

As time has passed, some Scriptures were altered and removed based on the prevailing attitudes at the time. This, in my opinion, provides room for our own interpretation of the Scriptures, regardless of which religion we may belong to. Being more knowledgeable today, we can reject what we believe is no longer applicable in our modern society.

Like everything else in this world, time also changes our religions, although some religions change faster than others. In the Protestant church in Norway, homosexuality was banned until just a few years ago. Now, homosexuals are accepted in this church community on equal terms with other people. This is a clear example of the fact that interpretations of the Scriptures change over time. If our religions don't change in line with the ever-increasing awareness of how things really are connected, I think our organised religions will gradually cease to exist.

If you are a non-believer, on the other hand, you may not have found this reading interesting. If this is the case, I encourage you to look into what makes you happy in your belief that there is no existence after death, and to keep your focus there.

You might feel relief to think there will be an end to all the suffering, having no hope or no interest in getting into a spin of new incarnations or living in a paradise, feeling bored for eternity. If a final death is a thought that makes you happy, your time on Earth has not been wasted, as your happiness is important not only for the quality of your life but also for the people who surround you. Who knows, maybe with time you will change your mind so that you, too, appreciate the thought of inner growth, change and eternal life ... And if not, maybe it really doesn't matter that much what happens in the future, as long as we feel good now.

In other words, we have the opportunity to choose between "Heaven" and "Hell" right here and now, based on what we choose to focus on. Abraham explains that our present is the only time we can really control. What happens in the future is created in the now before our future, making us the sole creators of our lives. Having said that, I do not believe in Hell. I just believe in contrast and imbalance; and imbalance is necessary for us to make new decisions so that we can change and move forward.

The crux of the matter is that, the more often we consciously choose a good thought, the more pleasant our lives will feel. Whether we choose to believe in a higher power or not, and whether we call this higher power the Source, God, Jehovah, or Allah does not matter. The thing that really, really matters is that *what* we choose to believe comforts us and gives us the opportunity to feel good.

LEARNING HOW TO MEDITATE

If you don't already know how to meditate, this is your chance to learn. Meditation was one of the main tools I used to get myself out of bed after I totally lost my energy and slept twenty hours a day.

Meditation is also a fantastic tool for gaining knowledge and an understanding of yourself and life in general. Through meditation, your energy level increases as soon as you let go of negative thoughts and change them with peace of mind. With a still mind, you are now able to listen to your inner being and its guidance.

Learning to meditate is easy. At first, you'll need the focus to sit for fifteen to twenty minutes every day, trying to leave out the chatter of your mind. The thoughts will come and go, and every time your thoughts start to jump around from one subject to another, you will need to focus your mind on your breath or a sound, etc. If you choose to meditate only now and then, it will be more difficult to get yourself into the flow.

There are many different techniques, and it's important to find one that suits you. The goal of meditation is to be able to access the stillness of your mind in your daily life so you don't always have to sit down to meditate to hear your inner being.

Today, I often find my mind quiets if I just focus for a couple of seconds on my breath while I'm going about my daily chores. Making myself conscious for a short while feels really, really pleasant. It's like floating on a cloud of stillness while refilling my body with peace, energy and knowledgeable guidance. However, to be able to get to this state and feel connected to our inner beings, we usually have to start our meditation practice while sitting.

The best time of day to meditate is immediately after you wake up in the morning; you can also meditate before going to bed. Setting your alarm clock fifteen to twenty minutes earlier in the morning and sitting up in bed with your hands resting on your thighs or folded as if in prayer is the easiest way. You could also find a chair, lie down or sit on the floor. Position yourself with your back straight to help you stay awake and to keep the chakras, or energy centres, in your torso open to allow the energy to flow freely.

It might be helpful to start your meditation practice slowly. For the first week, you can just sit for five minutes, the next week for ten, and then you should be ready to sit for fifteen to twenty minutes. If you are not able to meditate in the evening or the morning, find another time that suits you better. Or, if you can't sit for twenty minutes, sit for fifteen minutes. The most important thing is that you do it. Abraham recommends meditating every morning for fifteen minutes.

To help you focus on the stillness within, you can listen to the silence between or underneath the sounds in your room. Another technique is to focus on your breathing and your lungs and stomach moving up and down.

When I first started my meditation practice, I found it useful to count my thoughts, seeing how few thoughts I could have during my first minutes of a sitting, using this to be able to differentiate between a still and chatty mind.

Since then, I have learned how to distinguish between the thoughts I am thinking and the thoughts that are my inner being's guidance. The negative and worrying thoughts are mine, while the impulses and ideas that make me happy belong to my inner being.

Before going into meditation, state what you want to achieve. You might want to connect with your inner being, or you might just want to quiet the physical world and relax.

When you feel that your body goes numb, you know that you are experiencing meditation. The meditation experience can differ from person to person and from time to time, but there is no value in comparing our experiences. If you feel peace and numbness, that is enough.

On the Internet, you'll find a large selection of different meditation techniques. You can also visit my website.

For my part, I like Esther and Abraham's overall well-being meditation, where I focus on my breath. I "count" to three for each in-breath and "count" to five for every out-breath, while I listen effortlessly to Esther Hicks' voice and music in the background. (Go to the website, under "Feel Good," you will find a section for Abraham Hicks and Guided Meditation: **www.a-life-worth-living.org/guided-meditation**. You can also find Abraham Hicks on YouTube).

Kundalini yoga is another alternative to meditation. This type of yoga has also helped me to achieve inner peace. But it still requires that I meditate fifteen minutes each day if I really want to get good results.

A small warning: You will often feel negativity and bad feelings in the beginning after you get into a daily meditation routine, but don't worry. This is just a sign that you have begun to respond to the warnings that your inner being transmits to you. You will now feel disconnected every time you start thinking negative thoughts, which is a big advantage, as this warning allows you to consciously choose a new thought before your negativity attracts negative consequences. This is why it's not advisable to meditate inconsistently. It is similar to stopping physical exercise for a while and starting over again. You feel more pain.

You can compare the feelings of disconnection with the pain you feel when touching a hot oven. The body sends out signals that you'll damage your hand if you don't move it quickly from the heat. In the same way, your inner being gives you warnings through bad feelings when you think negative thoughts. It will then be easier for you to adjust your thoughts to avoid getting on a collision course with your dreams.

ASSIGNMENT 11

Find a meditation practice that works for you. In your journal, write down what you hope to achieve from your meditation practice. During the meditation though, it is important to relax and not have any expectations or requirements, but instead to be open and uncritical.

My Turn

What I Hope to Achieve from My Meditation Practice

I've tried out many techniques for meditation throughout the years. Some I liked, while others were not for me. In the beginning, I just meditated when I felt like it. Then I did it for a period of time, but fell out of the routine after a while. Sometimes I meditated alone, other times in groups. For me, it doesn't make a big difference if I meditate alone or with others. What did make a huge difference, though, was when I decided to meditate every day.

After some months of keeping my meditation routine, great ideas began to pop into my mind. It became easier to find solutions to problems, and my eyes started to open to all the "miracles" that surrounded me. The miracles might have been there anyway, but now, with a focused and still mind, I was able to recognise and appreciate them.

. . .

When I first started working with traumatised children in South-Sudan, I almost gave up. The children had been through so much violence, both physical and psychological, that they were not able to focus at all. They were screaming, yelling and fighting each other from when I entered the centre in the morning to when I left in the evening. If I tried to interfere, they would attack me too.

For months, I was only able to observe and protect the younger children from being attacked by the older ones. Rules, regulations or punishment for misbehaviour had no impact on these children.

Coming home from a rough day at the centre, I started to sit down and meditate. After some months, with focus on what I could do for these children, I came up with an idea of introducing Qigong. I wanted to help the children release heavy energy from their traumatised bodies and minds and, surprisingly, it worked like a charm.

Standing in a circle, the children were asked to shake their arms and legs while making grimaces and sounds that expressed their emotions. When the angry sounds began to slow down and soften, I would ask the children to lie on their backs and feel the blood circulating through their bodies. Then I would ask them to close their eyes while I took them to an imaginary world that they could enter every night after going to bed and make into their own secret place. Through the routine of taking their thoughts to their own secret place, the children learned to quiet their minds on their own.

After a short time, I was able to teach the children gratitude. In the beginning, they couldn't see that they had anything to be grateful for. Asking them to pick up a pencil on my desk without using their arms or legs proved them wrong. From here, I was able to teach them how to read and write.

Having my own reading and writing problems as a backdrop, I was also able to teach the children with learning difficulties how to read. When I left the centre three years later, these children behaved just like any other "normal" children, thanks to their new ability to still their minds and focus.

Your Turn

A. You might need some time to find a meditation technique that suits you. You might also find it difficult to sit still and focus. If this is the case, I can recommend doing a bit of Qigong or yoga first to be able to tune in to your body and mind.

Take a look at the "Feel Good" YouTube videos on this book's website under "Qigong" and "Yoga": www.a-life-worth-living.org/feel-good.

B. In your journal, write down what areas of difficulty you think your mediation practice may be able to help. After a few months of daily practice, you will discover that you can see your life more clearly, and from here you will be able to find solutions to your challenges.

> **MANTRA:** Being able to listen to the guidance of my inner being so that I can learn to be happy with myself and others is perhaps the most important goal in meditation.

RIGHT DECISIONS

It can be hard to make decisions in life, mainly because we don't know the consequences or outcomes of our decisions beforehand or because we are not sure what we really want. However, not making a decision is often worse than making the wrong decision, as it stops us from moving forward, allowing our lives to feel stagnant. Stagnant living is painful, because we feel we are not getting anywhere with our lives.

If we make the wrong decision, we can usually change our minds; however, the consequences of some decisions, such as deciding to have a baby, mean you're pretty much stuck when the baby is out there kicking and screaming. Whatever the decision might be, there is, however, always a way to get through it by either taking the consequences or bailing out.

Giving a baby away for adoption, getting a divorce or getting back to school and studying something that makes your life finally tick can be emotionally hard and also costly. This is why most of us want to do everything in our power to make our decisions right from the beginning, not having to go through these kinds of emotional difficulties.

Hence the question: **Is there a way of making sure that we are making the right decision?**

I believe all our decisions are right. Handling a sick body or going through a difficult marriage might be the eye-opener we have asked for, as all of our experiences, good and bad, are excellent teaching tools. Having said that, there are some shortcuts we can use to make sure we are moving ourselves in the right direction a bit faster.

By now you should know what shortcut I'm talking about. Do you remember? Right! You can choose to raise yourself to higher vibrations on the scale of emotions before making any decisions. The same tool works if you want to get back to a happy life after making a decision that hurt your feelings.

Soothing, gratefulness and meditation help both before you make a decision and after you have made a decision that triggers bad feelings. And they always work. If you are feeling anything less than happy, it's better to leave an important decision until you feel better.

Should you, on the other hand, feel a strong impulse to act on less important things in life, don't spend time thinking about it but follow your gut feeling. **It is through gut feeling that your inner being communicates with you to get you out of danger, help you meet the right person or get you into the right situation,** so you can live your dream.

If you want to make sure that an important decision is right, you can first lift your vibrations. Think about your choice and notice if this gives you a good feeling. If you feel good, you know that your choice correlates with your inner being's knowledge of what you dream about. If you feel unsure, you might be on a collision course with your dreams. Take some time to practise until you get to know your feelings. **If, even after a week, you feel good when thinking about your choice, you can be pretty sure your decision is correct.**

Sometimes we can feel frightened in view of the challenge we face. It may be a journey, a promise, or something else that we are uncertain about. The same tool can be used here. Make sure to get yourself up to the good feelings, as vibrating high will give you access to your inner being, which in turn will give you an objective picture of the situation and tell you if there is reason for your fear.

In order to get to know your feelings, you must nevertheless be willing to practise. You can do this by checking in with your inner being as often as you remember to. You make hundreds of decisions every single day, so there are plenty of opportunities to practise. The more conscious you become about what you want to achieve in each situation, the more control you'll have over your life.

Abraham recommends that we divide our days into segments. As we start each segment, we make ourselves aware of what we want to achieve.

The segments of your day will vary, but the first segment starts when you wake up in the morning. The next segment is often when you enter the bathroom. The next segment can be when you have breakfast. Maybe the next segment will be when you are traveling to work/school, and then the next segment will come when you meet people/colleagues/fellow students etc.

If you are not conscious before entering a new segment, you will leave your life to chance. When you are not conscious, you might fall victim to old habits where you think or talk about what you don't want instead of what you wish to achieve in the course of the day and in your life.

When you wake up in the morning, you can choose to visualise that this day is going well and tell yourself that everything is working out and that you have nothing to fear. When you go to the bathroom, you can make yourself conscious of being kind to your mirror image and being happy with your body. Before you eat breakfast, you can visualise that the food you give your body is good and beneficial. When you sit in the car or go out into traffic, you can visualise that you will have a nice time and arrive happy and satisfied. Before you meet other people, you can become aware of what you want to communicate and that you wish to be as uplifting, clear and constructive as possible.

• • •

Let us repeat what we have learned so far:

We now know that contrast teaches us to understand what we do not like, which in turn helps us to find out what we really like. As soon as you become aware of what you want from life, your wishes are recorded by your inner being. Your inner being then gives you directions through your feelings so that you will be able to experience your own growth, and thus live the life you wish for. The challenge is that you are only able to listen to directions when you vibrate high on your own emotional scale, as your inner being operates only from the high vibrations.

Abraham Hicks calls this place the **Vortex**, which is where all the positive things we want in life materialise from and where our inner being and the Source, in the non-physical, are located.

Everything in this world is made of energy. The energy takes shape through our thoughts, emotions and visualisations. By choosing to vibrate the energy at the top of the scale of your emotions, you will automatically be drawn into the Vortex, where your dreams are manifested.

In order to be able to extract your dreams so that you can experience them in your physical existence as well, you need to keep your feelings at the top of the emotional scale for enough time to allow your creations to materialise. When you become negatively focused, you stop the flow of good things coming your way and allow the lack of your dream to materialise instead. In this way, you close the door to your dream.

A life without learning and development isn't possible, although it may feel as if we aren't moving forward when we encounter one challenge after another. However, as soon as we understand that our mistakes give us important experiences, our learning will go much faster. We will then stop using energy on accusations, but rather concentrate on how this experience can be used as a springboard to reach new heights.

If you choose to spend a long time in a dark deep valley on your life journey, you can still reach your dream, but the dream will take longer to manifest itself. All roads will take you to your destination sooner or later. However, it may be a good idea to restart your journey if you aren't enjoying the place you have stopped.

We need fear to help us avoid dangerous situations. But when we lose contact with our inner being, we are unable to listen to our inner guidance. Then we will either get into a lot of trouble because we aren't listening to the warning bells we are receiving from our inner being, or we will get so used to being scared that we won't dare to live our lives because our focus is mainly on the negative thoughts and on everything that can go wrong.

ASSIGNMENT 12

In your journal, write down an example of a time where you made a decision out of fear and what the outcome was. Then do the same with a decision made out of joy.

My Turn

Making Decisions

Over time, I have realised that there is no purpose in regretting my bad decisions. However, there is great value in learning to see the consequences of my actions before I make a similar choice next time.

• • •

Deciding to leave South-Sudan for Ethiopia was a relief because the political situation in South-Sudan was getting worse and worse, but saying goodbye to the beautiful children to whom I had become so attached felt terrible.

The thought of starting my life from scratch in Ethiopia didn't feel appealing either. However, I knew from experience that, after a while, I would appreciate the opportunity to get to know new people and new cultures. And, since Ethiopia has a very old and fascinating culture, fantastic nature and beautiful people, I said yes when this opportunity came up.

A month before going to Ethiopia, I did an intuitive painting with an artist friend at home in Norway. Before we started to paint, we talked about Ethiopia and how I felt about going. I said I wasn't sure about how I felt, as some parts of me wanted to go and some parts wanted to stay in Norway with my friends and family.

When doing an intuitive painting, we usually start with a short meditation and then let our intuition do the work. This time, however, we didn't meditate. After half an hour or so, my friend stared at my picture and said, "Stop painting, Nina, and come and look at your work from a distance."

Stopping and gazing at my picture, I became conscious of what I was working on: it was my feelings about going to Ethiopia. At that moment,

I knew for sure that I was scared and didn't want to go. In the painting, I saw the sailing ships ready to leave the harbour waiting for the crack of dawn, and I felt a chill of fear and sadness run down my spine.

Over the following days I thought of bailing out of going to Ethiopia, but, after a meditation, I changed my mind again: I wanted to go.

What had happened to make me unsure about going was my discovery of how nice it was to work with like-minded friends. On the other hand, I knew that Ethiopia had something to offer and that I couldn't bail out, at least not at that moment.

What was interesting though was that my painting showed me that my interest in moving around the world had begun to fade, and that I would soon have to look into finding some roots and stability in my life. Despite my painting's message, as I sit here writing in the shade of an acacia tree in my lovely garden in Addis, I'm very happy that I said yes to another adventure in Africa. I already have interesting friends in the film world after volunteering at the Ethiopian International Film Festival. I've also gotten new writing skills from attending workshops at the festival, and I've been able to discover Ethiopia's fascinating culture from the inside.

In addition, living in Addis has given me time to read, write and paint, whereas staying home in Norway would have meant going back to my job at the university. Having a full-time job, I might not have had the time or the energy to do the things I love the most – at least, not as much as I would like to – and I'm not so sure if my soul would soar as much if I was sitting in an office in Norway as it does sitting here writing in my garden.

The challenge is that, when I choose to follow my husband on his assignments, it often brings us to vulnerable states with major political and social challenges. Yet it is not here that the greatest challenge for me lies personally. The most difficult thing for me is to say goodbye to all the wonderful people I've become so incredibly fond of.

For over thirty-five years, I've been on the move and have lived between three months and five years in each place. During these years, I have met and said goodbye to a lot of people. The paradox is that all of these amazing individuals and their exciting backgrounds and cultures are the reason why we choose to move on, as our ever-changing friendships and insight into new cultures enrich our lives.

How my stay here in Addis will end, I don't know at this moment. When I chose to move to Ethiopia, the country was peaceful. Now, Ethiopia is in a state of emergency. The Internet has been taken down, and for a while we were not allowed to travel more than four miles outside the capital, Addis Ababa. Before the state of emergency, hundreds of people were abducted, imprisoned and killed. Since the state of emergency was introduced, thousands have been imprisoned. However, it is quiet in the country. We can only hope that the authorities and the Ethiopian people will find peaceful solutions, despite their differing opinions on how to achieve growth and development.

• • •

What we often forget is that growth and development have no purpose if we don't understand that the goal of growth must be a freer, more loving and, therefore, a less painful world.

After all, it is our individual responsibility where we choose to keep our focus: on the good, constructive thoughts or the negative, destructive thoughts. Whatever we choose, it will have consequences. If we choose destructive thoughts, the choice will often be one of two: accept the challenge and stay, or flee from our problems.

If we choose to get to know our inner guide better, it will be much easier to make decisions with a happy outcome. However, there is no reason to worry about making the wrong choices. Looking at life from the perspective of eternity, we will all reach our goals and dreams, although by choosing to stay conscious more often, we'll reach our dreams faster.

Your Turn

My example is not the best, as my decision to go to Ethiopia was not made from pure joy or fear. Yet I chose this story because we often have mixed feelings when faced with a choice.

Your examples may be very personal, but your journal is just for you. So go ahead and pour them out on your white pages. Seeing the difference between making a decision out of fear as opposed to making a decision out of joy will convince you to spend a bit more time getting yourself into the Vortex before acting.

If you find it hard to think of an example, look at your religious belief and what kind of decisions you've made as a result of this belief.

> **MANTRA:** In every bad situation, there is an element of good.

—That's it for now.

NEXT TIME:

- How to deal with anxiety and depression
- How to look at suicide and death
- What is the right path?

FIFTH JOURNEY
TOGETHER

ANXIETY AND DEPRESSION

Many people suffer from anxiety and depression at some point in their lives. We are now going to discover how to quickly escape from this dark place.

I have personally been through the mild forms of depression without serious suicidal thoughts, and I know how to deal with such a condition. However, if you have suicidal thoughts, please do not follow my advice if it contradicts your doctor's recommendations.

Antidepressant drugs are often prescribed by doctors to get us out of the deep place where dark, heavy thoughts bother us. For people who are seriously ill, this is a good strategy. If you are suicidal, antidepressant drugs can prevent you from going so deeply down the emotion scale that you do not want to live anymore. Wanting to live is a prerequisite for being able to do something about your situation. Whether you are suicidal or not, do not do anything about your medication until you feel stable, happy and pleased with your life, and make sure that if you do something it is in consultation with your doctor.

If you do decide to reduce or stop your medication in discussion with your doctor, the process may take three to twenty-four months depending on how long you have been on the medication and how high your dose is. I would strongly advise you to have a good dialogue with your friends and family. Reducing this type of medication is a process where it is beneficial to have good support around you.

Below, you will be inspired to see your situation in a new light, whether you are on medication or not.

The reason for our depression doesn't have to come from just one situation, but is usually caused by a succession of events that finally get to be too much to handle. Analysing the problem is not the way, however, as going into the depths of the problem just keeps us there. Recognising what the depression stems from is good though, as we can then choose to see our life differently.

There are so many reasons for us to become depressed: growing up with parents who are depressed; losing a loved one or a job; health issues or being abused; feeling that life just sucks, or worse, that we suck; feeling like we don't get anything right; feeling like everybody else is so successful and beautiful, but not us. The list is endless.

You might think that the source of your depression is "out there," as you might have lost a loved one or been abused, and that what happened to you is not just a thought. Whatever it is that caused your depression, it doesn't matter, as everything can be handled in the way you think and feel about it.

So, let's get to work.

Make a list of things that you believe are the cause of your depression and, for each thing, ask yourself:

1. How can I look at my situation differently?

It can be hard to do this task if something really bad has happened to you. If you are still asking yourself, "How is it possible to look at my situation differently?" listen to Nick Vujicic one more time: **www.a-life-worth-living.org/feel-good/inspiration**.

Then you can ask yourself:

2. Do my thoughts serve me anymore?

Do my thoughts cheer me up, or do they take me down? If you grew up with parents who were depressed, you might have "inherited" their heavy view of life. But, through exercises, it is possible to learn to consciously shift the focus by choosing better thoughts and another way of seeing life. Whatever the reason for your depression, ask yourself if your thoughts are worth focusing on.

3. Will my life get any better if I am depressed about my situation?

Am I able to see that I have a choice between thinking the same thoughts and staying where I am and choosing to change the way I think and get a new life?

4. Do I believe in the Law of Attraction?

Am I able to see that I have the power, through my own thoughts and feelings, to attract both good and bad situations, depending on where on the scale of emotions I choose to be?

Or have I dug such deep, negative "ditches of thought" in my brain that I can no longer manage to see the positive aspects of my life, despite the fact that they are actually there?

5. What benefits have I derived from being depressed?

Surprisingly, you might find that you have gained quite a few benefits:

people might feel sorry for you; you might get more attention; you don't need to be responsible for your actions to the same extent; you might get time off from school or work or other chores.

6. Do I believe that these benefits will bring me happiness?

7. Would I prefer to be a victim?

...And believe that every nasty thing can be thrown at me for no reason at all, or do I instead want to believe that I'm responsible for everything that happens to me, both good and bad? In the case of the latter, ask yourself:

8. How can I take charge of my own situation and get out of this depressive dump?

The answer is through one thought at a time, up the scale of emotions. Soothing, gratitude and meditation are all great tools you now know how to use.

(Still, remember not to get angry with yourself on the days you fail and do not manage to see anything positive in your life.)

> **MANTRA:** It's not what happens to me, but how I react to it that matters.

THE SAME GOES FOR ANXIETY.

First of all, ask yourself if it serves you to hold on to the fear. If you have decided to get rid of it, follow the recipe below:

Choose to stop anxiety a long time before it hits you by deciding to start your day consciously from the moment you open your eyes.

Now you are prepared. When you feel the anxiety coming, focus on your breath. Breathe deeply in, as you slowly count to three. Breathe out, while counting to five. When you feel more relaxed, change your mind to something nice or something you're grateful for. By deliberately shifting focus to good thoughts and your breath, you now also have a tool for controlling anxiety.

The challenge with anxiety is that we often try to avoid situations that can put us out of balance. Unfortunately, if we are not willing to challenge ourselves, no change will happen. In a situation where you want to avoid challenging yourself, remember that anxiety is just a thought that you can control by consciously choosing something else to think about that will make you feel good.

Here your mantras can really become helpful:
If others can do it, then I can do it as well. It's probably not as bad as I first thought. Even if something went wrong for someone else, it's unlikely that it will go wrong for me.

You now have a tool for the main types of anxiety. All you have to do is practise by challenging yourself. And if you do, I promise you that your new tool will help you.

This may sound very simple, but if you suffer from severe anxiety, you may feel so weak that you cannot grasp yourself and bring about change without outside help.

If you suffer from a very strong and paralysing anxiety, you can go to my website, **www.a-life-worth.living.org**. Under "Health," you will find a professional website for anxiety. You can also use the forum on the website and check up there if anyone can support you. Or if you have someone around you – friends or family or a teacher, doctor or psychologist – that you feel confident in, please let them know that you need help.

ASSIGNMENT 13

A. In your journal, write down the answers to the questions above.

B. Create a good routine for food, sleep, nature walks, social activities and work. Write it out and stick it on your wall, where you can see it each morning. Tell people around you so they know what to expect.

C. Then write down what your dream life looks like. Write in the present tense, as if it is already happening. You don't need to suffer from depression or anxiety to do this exercise.

My Turn

A. Overcoming My Depression and Anxiety

I have finally overcome my depression and anxiety and now live life mostly in excitement and joy. In spite of this, my thoughts still create fear and depressive feelings inside me. As soon as I am conscious of the negative feelings, however, I try to choose to see my situation from a better and more positive angle.

The next image shows when the idea of writing this guide was created. I had finally managed to get through the narrow, pitch-black cave behind me without feeling fear. I didn't feel anxiety from looking down the steep mountain cliff in front of me, either. At that moment, I knew that, in addition to overcoming my depression and fatigue, I had overcome my

fear of heights and dark claustrophobic places that had so long paralysed
me. That was when I thought that my
story might be of help to others who
were struggling, as I did, to find a way
out of the dark.

C. My Dream Life

The sun rises up, red and ripe, from
the blue, velvety sea to the east, while
the full moon descends behind the
majestic mountain range in the west. I cheerfully stroll up the soft, sandy
beach, experiencing another magical birth of a new day.

My little world is still in a state of silent drowsiness, apart from a few
chirping early birds. My dog, who's wagging his tail, runs towards the
house in the direction of his water bowl. I turn around to take one last
glance over the ocean and the dimly blushing morning sky before I enter
the house to make coffee.

Soon after, I'll come out with my coffee cup in one hand and the laptop
in the other. I'm sitting in the garden hammock on the porch, squinting thoughtfully over the ocean. While I take a sip of coffee, I smile at
the sun. "Thank you for warming me and for lighting up my life," I think
happily. I take another sip of the coffee and open the laptop to find the
fairy-tale I'm working on.

Theodor, my dog, lies at my feet and starts licking me between my toes.
"I'm finally living my dream," I say to myself while gently patting Theodor
on his back. My thoughts return to that moment outside the dark, narrow cave when the idea of *The Guide to A Life Worth Living* came to me.

One grateful thought leads to the next, and I begin to reflect on life and everything that has happened in recent years. I get up thoughtfully to fetch my diary. I think this is a good time to write a brief overview of the years that have passed since I started this process:

Over the last ten-year period, in fact, everything has gone according to plan. The family often gathers despite the fact that we are spread throughout the globe. My work has gained the recognition that I have long dreamed of and is now being read by people on all continents. My health is excellent; I feel strong and energetic. In addition, my blood sugar is well under control as a result of a conscious focus on a healthy and happy body.

As my life is now, it could not be better. I have finally reached the top of the mountain range that I have planned to climb ever since I was just a young girl. Getting up here has been challenging, but incredibly rewarding. I really feel great joy and gratitude towards my new life.

My income is sufficient, which means I can focus on what really interests me. In recent years, I have built up a rehabilitation centre combined with a research centre where the focus is on finding solutions to mental challenges. I have linked up with the university in my city, where we test techniques that can help people with thought disturbances to master their lives.

The research results prove to be extremely good and the interest in our work has been enormous. Recently, we presented the latest research findings that confirm that our thoughts can make us healthy or sick, depending on if the thoughts raise the mood of the mind or drag it down the scale of emotions. We have also managed to confirm that our feelings have the ability to attract both good and bad situations, depending on what thoughts we choose to focus on.

As I close my diary, my grandchild, Emma, comes out of the doorway with her toy rabbit in her hand, his ears slowly sweeping the wooden floor. "Are you up already, Grandma?" she asks and walks, still sleepy, towards me in the garden hammock. (Just to remind you, I'm still writing about my dream life.)

I nod and lift her up on my lap. "Yes, sweetie. I thought I would write a new chapter of our fairy-tale, but first I needed to write down some thoughts in my diary."

"Will Graff the Giraffe be happy at last?" she asks, and puts herself in the crook of my arm.

"Yes, everyone will be fine, Graff included. You see, soon Graff will learn to focus on the good things in his life and what he really, really wants instead of focusing on what he hates and doesn't like, and you know what will happen then?" I smile and kiss my granddaughter tenderly on her cheek.

Emma glances up at me and nods eagerly. "Graff will attract the good things and he will finally be happy."

"That's right!"

My granddaughter's drowsiness is now gone. "Easy peasy, in other words," she suddenly exclaims, and throws her toy rabbit high up in the air.

I am enjoying Emma's eagerness and I hug her happily. "Graff will be fine again, but first he has to learn the tricks and be willing to practise, and this is where the challenge lies!"

Emma looks, frustrated, up at me. "Why do you always have to make it so difficult, grandmother?"

"It's not so difficult, Emma, but all the things we're going to learn take some time. However, Graff is not willing to learn, do you remember?"

Emma nods sadly. "But couldn't we make him want to learn?"

"We can't force anyone to learn, but we can try to inspire," I explain.

Emma jumps down from my lap and picks up her bunny before she turns to ask me, "What if we let someone come and talk to Graff?"

"Good idea!" I reply and open the laptop. Emma places herself next to me in the hammock. "Who do you think should visit Graff?" I ask and get ready to write.

"Someone from the same island?" Emma answers confidently.

I nod, "Someone who knows how it is to lose their family and who speaks the same language as Graff?" Emma agrees and hugs her bunny, excited.

Graff the Giraffe and his two helpers

Your Turn

Answer all the questions above and then write a paragraph in your journal about what kind of life you want to live, using the present tense. If you take your time doing these exercises, when this journey is over, your journal will be a witness to your great growth.

MANTRA: If others can make it, so can I.

SUICIDE AND DEATH

You might find this topic depressing and even morbid; however, death, as we understand it, is often the reason why we are too scared to live our lives to the fullest.

Death is inevitable, while living is a choice. Choosing to get the most out of our lives is difficult if we are always guarding against death.

Since I could walk, I've been hearing warnings from family and friends. "Be careful!" "Don't do that, it can kill you!" All the advice I got was meant to protect me from harm; however, it also made me worried about death. It didn't make sense to me that there should be such beautiful stories about Heaven, yet such dire warnings about ending up there.

As I grew older, I started to compare my life and death to the cycle of a flower that retreats for the winter and then flowers again the next spring or summer. After listening to Abraham though, I gained an even better understanding of death, which I'd like to share with you, as this understanding has allowed me to dare to live my life to the fullest. I hope it will also be helpful to you.

Abraham says that there is no death, as we are all eternal beings. When we leave our bodies, it's just a transition from physical form to non-physical form. The largest part of us is always in the non-physical though, so when we take on a body for a new ride, the larger part, our soul or inner being, will stay behind in the non-physical, guiding us.

Furthermore, our inner being is a part of the Source. In this way we are all part of "All That Is" and much, much bigger than we think. This means that our physical body is only a tiny part of us.

When we die, we just withdraw our consciousness from the body, and there's no more to it than what we do every time we go to sleep, except that we now leave the body behind for good. Before entering our new life, we have already decided on some of the challenges we would like to experience and learn from, and sometimes these experiences are painful.

Because of the Law of Attraction, nobody can kill anybody. We all are responsible for what happens to us. Every death can therefore be interpreted as a suicide, as it's our own thought and focus that attracts what's happening to us. If we are negatively focused or frightened by life, the chance that we attract situations that give us more to be negative and frightened about is much greater.

If someone decides to take their own life, they end their life in a more deliberate way. Leaving the body deliberately, they join the pure positive energy that is their inner being, and they close the gap between themselves and the Source.

The Source will never despise us for deliberately closing this gap, as this is the gap we try to close every time we choose good feelings instead of bad. However, when we eagerly jumped into our bodies for a new ride, we all did it with the intention of reaching our goals. Some chose a harder ride than others though, and might need a helping hand to get through the dark places before reaching the lighter ones. Nevertheless, some choose such an unbearable pain that a hand to hold is not soothing enough and, in that case, they might bail out.

If we choose to help people who are suffering, going down to the emotional level of the person in need is not the way. Instead, we should help from our place in the Vortex (high vibrations), knowing that if we leave our place of happiness we can help no one. When we feel sorry for someone and get stressed or anxious about their situation, we have nothing to give; instead, we just add more power to the problem, which means we move ourselves and the person in need even further from a solution.

However, if we are to see a person for who he or she really is, namely an extension of the Source, there is no need to worry, as we all go in and out of balance. We can show empathy, but we need to keep calm. Imbalance is, as we know, essential for all of us to expand and develop.

If I had had this knowledge as I grew up, I believe my life would have been quite different. But I didn't. Instead, I learned the hard way, using all my energy getting upset and worrying, making my own situation and others' much worse than they originally had to be. On the other hand, none of us are perfect, and there's no harm in getting out of balance, as long as we remember to move forward and find new balance. Nor is there a crisis if we die, as we will forever go in and out of our physical existence.

ASSIGNMENT 14

In your journal, write down your experience with death and suicide. How can this new understanding help you live a richer life?

My Turn

My Experience with Death and Suicide

When I was eleven, my parents built a cottage by the fjords in the southern part of Norway, and my life as a nomad began. All of our free time was spent at the cottage, which meant I had double sets of everything, including friends.

At the cottage, I met a boy a few years younger than me who became one of my dearest friends. What I liked best about my new friend was that he was really excited about life and loved adventures. We did a lot of exciting things together, including building a raft, sailing on the fjord, collecting crabs by torchlight during the night, and getting lost in the mountains and having the whole village search for us.

At seventeen years old, I met my first boyfriend. Going to the cottage was not a priority anymore so, when my parents went, I chose to stay home. I kept in contact with my friend via mail, however, and he once came to visit me in my hometown.

After getting married, my husband and I decided to study in the United States for a few years. Before leaving, I visited my friend after not seeing him for many years. This was when he told me he had become ill. He heard voices, and these voices made him go totally nuts. I felt so bad about leaving my friend behind, as I thought I might be the only one who could really help him. But he insisted that I go. Before leaving, I made him promise to contact his doctor and tell his parents about his problems. He did, and he ended up in a psychiatric ward a few weeks later.

I communicated with my friend by mail and tried my best to find new research on schizophrenia at the local library in the United States, as the hospital in Norway could not find any schizophrenia medication that could mute the voices in my dear friend's head. However, my research didn't yield any results.

One day I got a letter from a nurse telling me that my friend had lost his eyesight due to side effects of his medication. My friend had also tried to commit suicide several times but had been saved.

I felt devastated by this news and, not being able to communicate with my friend anymore, I didn't know what to do. Finally, I came up with the idea of recording my voice. When I was on my own, I recorded the sounds of daily life, with me talking in the background, reminding my friend of all the good things about life.

I recorded the birds in the park and the sounds at the supermarket, telling my friend how different everything was here compared to the village at home. I reminded him about all the good times we had had together, about the future and about all the new discoveries in the world of medicine.

Finally, one day I received a letter addressed in the handwriting of my friend. I tore open the letter and eagerly started to read. Surprisingly, he told me he felt much better; the doctors had taken him off the medication and sent him home. His eyesight was back and he was planning to take an offshore job.

I had already told my friend about my plan to travel the world. Actually, we were just leaving our apartment as I received the letter from the mail carrier.

Excited and grateful, I shared the good news with my husband as I picked up my backpack from the ground. My friend wished us an exciting trip and said he would be with me every step of my journey. What he meant by this remark, I didn't understand – not yet.

In every new place we visited around the world, I wrote a postcard to my friend. When we landed safely in Norway six months later, my mother told me, on the way home from the airport, that my friend had committed suicide. The last letter he had written was the one I had received just before leaving the United States.

My first reaction was total disbelief. How was it even possible? I had sent a dozen postcards to my dead friend and no one had told me the sad news when I, on several occasions, had called home. After the feeling of disbelief, I became furious. "Why? Why didn't you tell me?" I yelled at my mother. My mother turned around slowly from the front passenger seat to face me. "We expected you to take it very hard, so we decided not to tell you until you came home. If we had told you, it might have ruined the journey of your dreams," my mother answered. "I'm so, so sorry."

My parents wanted to take me to my friend's grave, but I refused. "He's not there, anyway," I said to my parents. Instead, I walked to the favourite places where my friend and I had had so much fun growing up together. Sitting on our favourite spot on the mountain overlooking the fjord, I started to blame myself for leaving my friend when he needed me most, and this feeling of guilt and sadness stayed with me for years and years.

However, with my new understanding of death, I've stopped blaming myself. I now doubt that I could have prevented my friend from committing suicide. I was not prepared for that kind of job, as most of the time when I thought of my friend I went down to the basement, to the low vibrations. Not being able to keep myself in the Vortex in the long run, I might not have been of much help after all.

None of us are responsible for how another person chooses to tackle their life. We are responsible only for our own.

Believing that we are all going in and out of physical existence, getting new chances to reach the goals we make for ourselves, I no longer feel as sad when people die. I will miss them though, just as I miss all my friends when I have to say goodbye. With the "dead" ones, on the other hand, I've started to feel they are always with me. I remind myself that, before leaving his body, my dear friend wrote me, "I will be with you every step of your journey," and I really believe that he is.

Your Turn

In your journal, write about your own experience with death and suicide, if you have one. With your new knowledge, see if you are able to change your view on these subjects and make your life easier to live.

> **MANTRA:** My soul or inner being is by far the largest part of me. It is always there in the non-physical to guide me. However, it is up to me, in physical life, to decide whether I will choose to listen to my inner being and the inspiration and impulses I am constantly given through my feelings.

THE RIGHT PATH

Maybe we should ask again: Is there a right path? Yes. All of them are right. If you look back, you'll discover that you needed all the turns and backtracks in your life to be just where you are today, and where you are today is the perfect starting point for the rest of your journey.

You might think that where you are today is a place you'd rather not be. Then you forget that where you are today is just a passing point; it doesn't have to be your final destination. The less you dwell in the place you dislike, the more quickly you'll reach the place of your liking.

The right path is the one that makes you happy. That being said, some people will choose shortcuts, while others will choose detours. Some will also unconsciously choose to stay in a place they dislike for a long time, rather than moving on. Furthermore, what makes us happy will change over time.

When we are very young, we might find it fun to jump into puddles. When we are older, we might enjoy playing games. As adults, we might enjoy building a home. Abraham explains that, from one moment to the next, what we enjoy doing will change, just like the scenery changes on our journey from one city to the next.

When you feel unhappy where you are, the best idea is to find out what will make you happy and head there instead. The challenge is that we are not always aware that we can actually choose to get on with our lives. As a result, we get stuck in a place of unhappiness.

Just as everything else in this world is changing, we are also changing. A place we used to love might now make us bored or sad, and it may be time to continue our journey. By monitoring our feelings, we can lay the path for our journey one feeling at a time. Our feelings will immediately tell us if we have stopped at a place that is not to our liking.

If you have been unhappy for a long time, it just means it's high time to move forward. You are out of balance and you need to find a new balance. As long as you feel good, you know that you are growing and changing. If you are unhappy, you feel stagnated. If you feel stagnated, you just need to move yourself to a better-feeling place, and there you go.

When you arrived in this life, you knew what would make you happy. Being able to remember this, you can easily choose the thoughts and activities that will make your soul soar. If you don't remember, your happy feelings will easily guide you there.

Happiness is both your path and your goal, as this way you can move the world to a better place, not only for yourself, but for us all.

ASSIGNMENT 15

In your journal, write down some examples of times when you have stopped at a place not to your liking and how you felt when you decided to move on to a better place.

My Turn

Stopping at a Place Not to My Liking

For me, going home, taking an office job and not having the time or energy to write or travel feels like I'm not using my life. Becoming older, however, I now find too much traveling exhausting, and I have realised it will soon be time to find a new balance.

Life is always changing, and we need to change with it in order not to feel stagnated. This means that there is not only one big goal in life, but many different goals. If you follow your bliss, inspiration and happy feelings, you are sure to be on the "right" path.

Your Turn

The reason for doing these assignments is that writing your thoughts down in your journal makes you much more focused and conscious than when you just think through a situation. It also gives more power to your thoughts.

> **MANTRA:** If I follow my feelings of joy, excitement and inspiration, I can be sure to stay on the "right path."

—That's it for now.

NEXT TIME:

- Why are some people born homosexual?
- Why do we see so much turmoil in the world?
- What causes extreme weather?

SIXTH JOURNEY TOGETHER

HOMOSEXUALITY

Before entering this physical experience, I believe we make a decision about what we'd like to explore, learn, teach and work on to make the universe expand while we're here on Earth. The reason why some people choose to enter this world as homosexuals is to help us to accept diversity.

The more diverse our world becomes, the more expansion we'll see. Our pain will create a longing for change, and change will create new expansion. **If we all thought the same, looked the same and acted in the same way, change and growth would be much, much slower.**

To choose to enter this world being different from the "norm" is very brave, especially as you don't remember why you made the choice. And this goes for all types of not-the-norm roles we might have taken on, not only homosexuality.

The Source did not make only one type of flower or one type of bird. On Earth, we see huge diversity, even within the same species. It was never the intention to make the world homogenous; however, that is often the goal we make for ourselves. We want our children to fitt into the accepted norms of our society because we believe it will make life easier for them, and also easier for us. The leaders of our world also want their people to conform, as it's much easier to rule a group of people who behave within a given set of rules.

However, this was not the intention for life on Earth. **Acceptance and the feeling of joy of living in a diverse world are the goals.** Just imagine if all people looked like Barbie and Ken and everyone behaved in the same way. Imagine if all food tasted the same, if there was only one type of car, one type of house, one type of flower, one type of bird and one type of tree. How incredibly boring life would be! The sooner we can enjoy diversity, the sooner life on Earth will feel like a blessed placed to be. It's only our belief in sameness and conformity that keeps us from feeling joy here and now.

ASSIGNMENT 16

In your journal, write down some examples of people's traits that you dislike and why you don't like them. Try to see these people in a different light, with the knowledge of diversity being part of our goal, and see how you feel now.

My Turn

People's Traits That I've Found It Difficult to Like

My first introduction to homosexuality happened very early in life, as my best friend's uncle is homosexual. Sitting at the dinner table, I remember my friend and I found it very amusing to watch my friend's uncle's partner putting a serviette on the uncle's lap, telling him in a thin feminine voice to be careful not to ruin his new pair of trousers. Our amusement was, however, not judgemental, only surprised and joyful. That my friend's family behaved in a happy and non-judgemental way towards the homosexual couple meant I didn't find homosexuality strange at all.

Where I live in Addis, my neighbour's son's behaviour is very different from what I'm used to. In the beginning, I found it terribly annoying to listen to his angry shouts and screams from morning to evening as he refused to conform to his parent's way of life. After discovering that the little boy might be autistic, I started to look at him as a blessing and a teacher of diversity, and my annoyance is now gone.

Your Turn

Even though homosexuality has more or less been legally accepted in the western world, there are still countries in Africa, Asia and the Middle East where people are imprisoned and even killed for their sexual preferences. If you are struggling to accept your sexual preferences, think about yourself as a speaker of diversity. This way, you might see your sexual preference differently.

By choosing to think differently by heightening your feelings, you'll certainly attract situations from the station where good things in life are broadcast. Remember, by accepting yourself, you'll also become a good example for others.

> **MANTRA:** My special character is a tool for acceptance of diversity, no matter what this particular character may be.

TURMOIL AND TERRORISM

Most turmoil and terrorism are caused by our inability to accept diversity, believing that there's only one right way to worship, one right way of behaving and one right solution to any problem.

How many times have we been willing to put ourselves in other people's shoes and see life from their perspective? Very, very few, as far as I've observed. When we need to be right and have everyone act the way that pleases us, it's no wonder we see so much turmoil in our world. The world is not meant to conform.

If we look within our own families, we see the same patterns of forcing family members to conform, not to mention how we try to adapt to various trends in order to gain acceptance.

In the western world, we observe an increasing frequency of eating disorders, anxiety and depression. And why is that? It's because of our belief in rules made by others deciding how we should live and look, what is healthy, what is good behaviour and what is not acceptable. Gradually, the number of rules introduced exceed our ability to follow them all.

In addition, these unwritten laws are pushed on us from all directions, through parents, teachers, religion, advertising and the media. Finally, we bend to the unwritten rules. No one needs to dictate or yell at us any longer when we don't obey, as we have become sufficiently indoctrinated to blame ourselves when we aren't good enough or when we don't live up to the standards.

If we don't conform, we can feel like losers, and most of us dislike this feeling, as we are brought up believing in conformity. Being different from what our society accepts can cause lots of problems. We may become depressed or try our best to fit in by talking about what everyone else is concerned with, slim ourselves, interest ourselves in the same activities or get the right style and the right clothes. We may feel that, whatever we do, we will never completely fit in, and because it's not possible to keep up with our society's unwritten rules, we may feel that something is wrong with us. Some people feel so outside their society that they deliberately choose to end this journey.

There is no reason to worry though: to make an omelette, we need to break a few eggs first. And the "breaking the eggs" part is what we are busy working on now. As soon as people become conscious and accept themselves for who they are and put focus on what makes them happy while allowing others to do the same, we'll see change for the better.

We have been through the same process countless times before in the history of man. Just take a look at how we treated witches, Jews, blacks and communists. Fortunately, we learn from our mistakes. History appears as if it is constantly repeating itself. However, if we look closely, we will always find a new twist.

The eggs that are broken these days may not carry a "witch" stamp, but instead they are stamped with "terrorist," "gay," "Muslim," "foreigner" and others. Many eggs are destroyed in the process of change and expansion, which has been necessary as it is only through our mistakes and imbalances that we feel the pressure to find a new balance so we can move ourselves and our world forward.

However, it's now time to learn from our mistakes so we don't have to go through so much pain in the future. Currently, it may seem that the world is on its way back to a dead end, but the consequences of our actions and our strong longing for change will soon move us forward again.

The two main reasons we still experience so much turmoil in the world are that we have not yet realised that diversity is necessary for our development and that we do not yet understand the value of keeping ourselves conscious so we can learn more quickly from our mistakes.

If you'd like to see expansion, you need to be part of the change. With your feelings as your guide, you came here to explore, learn and teach, allowing Earth to evolve. To move forward though, you need to get out of balance first, and that's another reason why we see turmoil. The next step is to find a new balance, and on and on it goes. This means that there is no reason to worry. It's much more productive to focus on your own growth and to change yourself than to try to make everyone around you conform to please you.

Hopefully we will soon understand that we can't change anything for the better using fear as a weapon. War against crime, drugs and terrorists – or anything else for that matter – doesn't take us anywhere, but love does, Abraham explains.

Love heals everything while fear just makes things worse. When we learn to focus on what makes us happy as individuals and allow everybody else to do the same, we will be able to move both the world and ourselves to a more peaceful place.

ASSIGNMENT 17

Write down a few examples of where you can be the change in this world.

My Turn

Where I Can Be the Change in This World

As I've started focusing on creating a conscious, good and meaningful life,

I try to monitor my own feelings, knowing that when I'm feeling good, I'm evolving and changing and have not rooted myself at a point on my journey where I don't want to stay.

When I find myself feeling bad, I try to soothe myself up the scale of emotions or find something to do to distract me from having bad thoughts. If somebody really annoys me, I try to put myself in their shoes. If they still annoy me, I know that I've attracted the situation to myself and I try to see the other person through the eye of the Source.

When my husband annoys me, I remind myself of a photo of him as a child where he is sad but extremely cute. Often this picture helps me to see my husband's inner child and prevents me from staying annoyed with him.

When I worry about my children, I try to remind myself that they have their own lives to live and, if they want my advice, they will ask. But this is a tough one. Being a mother, I want my children to have good lives, and I want to do everything in my power to prevent them from having bad experiences. However, sheltering my children from life is not my job; they also need to lose their balance in order to move forward. Giving them a tool that can enable them to handle their own lives might be good, but giving them anything that is not asked for has little use.

I do ask my children to remind me of my own teaching when I lose my balance, though. Trying to be a good role model is perhaps my best contribution to change in this world. However, if my goal is to be perfect, and if I can't forgive others and myself for mistakes, I will only be draining myself of energy. Being perfect is a completely impossible task. The goal must therefore be to do my best with where I am at all times.

Your Turn

I believe we all have potential for new growth. If not, we wouldn't be here. Find a few places in your life where you believe that you can be the change.

MANTRA: Through my own example, I can help move the world into a better place for us all.

EXTREME WEATHER AND DISASTERS

Abraham Hicks says that the Earth doesn't need to be saved, but that it is perfect as it is. Abraham also says that humanity is just like a group of small fleas on the wide back of Mother Earth and will not be able to cause a big impact on the planet in the long-term – but humans can make Earth unpleasant to live on.

Everything in the universe is energy that is perfectly connected. The storms are there to move moisture to areas that need water. Water, but also droughts, gives life to humans, plants, birds, animals and insects. Temperatures have risen and descended through billions of years and, as a consequence, the Earth has gone in and out of ice ages and warm periods. The changes in temperatures have given people the opportunities to move to new areas on our planet.

Despite the fact that the Earth would survive new fluctuations in temperatures, our way of thinking will still enhance our personal experience of our life on Earth.

Very few people understand that our thoughts manifest themselves and take the form of positive or negative consequences, depending on what we choose to focus on. The more we focus on problems and forget to look for solutions, the more we experience problems around us.

In fact, taking care of our planet by not contaminating the air, the water and the ocean has finally started to become part of our common sense as a consequence of accelerated climate change. This shows us that everything in the universe is moving towards improvement and that the contrast we experience is helping us to make new and better choices as we, and our Earth, evolve.

The media's fearsome focus on disasters, weather and climate change is, however, not the way, as this negative focus will only drain us of energy.

If we instead choose to focus on the indescribably beautiful planet we are all part of and decide to find a balance that allows both humans and nature to thrive, our gratitude and love for nature and humanity will eventually lead to good and holistic solutions. (Be inspired by David Attenborough's documentary from 2019 and his proposed solutions.)

Disasters and climate change, on the other hand, will always be a part of our experience here on Earth, as these episodes also provide the basis for growth and expansion.

Everything in our world is in motion. Earthquakes, storms, floods, droughts, fires and epidemics play a central role in shaping, developing and changing our planet.

When people die in a disaster, we can choose to remind ourselves that if we leave our body, it is our own choice. We are just not always conscious enough to understand that our inner beings want a break from their physical experience and will step aside to let other souls get a chance to make their discoveries here on Earth.

Abraham says that we, as individuals, are able to create the lives we want regardless of the choices of others. We are given full freedom to choose how we want to live our lives. We have so much freedom that we can even choose captivity.

The challenge is that very few of us believe in our invincible inner power, and we often end up creating disasters in our own lives. The interesting thing is that, in time, disasters will steer us towards better solutions.

ASSIGNMENT 18

Write down a few examples of where you have seen people unaffected when they were in the middle of a disaster. If you have no experience of disasters, you can look at accidents such as car crashes, house fires or epidemics.

With this assignment, I wish to illustrate that many people are not affected even though they may be in the midst of disasters. Should we be affected, the disaster will eventually give rise to new growth. However, it may take time before we see this growth and learn from our mistakes. But no matter how long we need, seen from an eternal perspective, we will all eventually learn from our mistakes. This means that our concerns are largely groundless. Instead, they only drain energy and, as a consequence, our personal development is slower than it needs to be.

My Turn

An Example of Me Being in the Middle of a Disaster

I was alone in my home in South Africa when the biggest mountain fire ever swept over Cape Town. On the day of this worst-ever fire, I sat on my terrace trying to calm down my feelings while watching the smoke and fire move towards my house. Luckily for me, the wind was in favour of my house and the flames progressed only slowly in my direction.

Firefighters and helicopters were brought in from all over South Africa to fight the fire. As the flames were not stoppable in the strong wind, after a few days Desmond Tutu came on the radio, leading a prayer in which he asked for rain. That evening, rain and thunder broke loose. Ironically, the rain brought lightning that caused a new fire to flare up on the other side of my house, and this time the wind direction was not in my favour. The distance was far, but, with the strong wind, it could have reached my house within a day or so.

Thousands of people were evacuated from their homes as the smoke and fire came closer and closer. My house is built in the middle of the firebreak, high up in the mountains. Being located so high up, I wasn't affected by the smoke. However, my house would have been one of the first to go had the fire reached my village.

I was talking with my husband on the phone several times a day as he followed the news from South-Sudan. He was very worried and nervous, so I asked him to stop calling me, as he was also making me worried. Instead, I asked him to make sure the house was well-enough insured and then relax.

During the night, I kept the curtains open to follow the flames as they came closer. At the same time, I tried to stay calm, trusting that everything would be fine by the end of the night. In the morning, the fire had changed direction and my house was no longer in danger.

Only a few houses burned down in that huge fire. In Cape Town, people expect mountain fires every fifth year, as this is the way the special fynbos vegetation is able to regenerate itself. This makes the people behave in a calm and relaxed way, but they are always prepared for fires.

Sometimes we can attract a disaster to ourselves, not understanding what we have done to attract it, as my brother did when his farm burned down some years ago. Since my brother didn't have proper insurance on the farm, this really felt like a disaster for our family, but only until my brother decided to build a rehabilitation centre out of the little insurance money he did receive. This rehabilitation centre became a blessing from above, as it gave my brother a life mission that really makes his life worth living. (If you wonder, I just have one sibling, and he is very dear to me).

Your Turn

We see the teaching of keeping calm and trusting our own power in many fairy-tales, as many storylines tell us that if we are brave, we'll conquer our obstacles no matter how scary they might be.

Consciously choosing to think positive, loving and constructive thoughts will lead to positive, loving and constructive actions that in turn will affect us, nature and everything around us. Conscious thoughts are therefore also important in terms of climate change and disasters.

Should you have ideas on how we can find solutions to our challenges, join the competitions that are posted on the website: **www.a-life-worth-living.org/global-issues/**.

> **MANTRA:** Fear drains my energy, while faith in my inner power makes me invincible.

HALFWAY THROUGH OUR JOURNEY

If you have done all your assignments, you will by now feel new empowerment, as your life is hopefully much more interesting and meaningful than it was before you started this journey.

Growing and changing is fun, but also challenging. Sometimes it's hard to pull ourselves forward, however, it's undoubtedly worth it. Nevertheless it's up to each one of us to choose when we'd like to move forward with our lives. Self-discovery is not something we can push onto others. To be willing to invest time into conscious living, we usually need to feel a deep longing for change. Today, I'm so grateful for all of my challenges, as without them I would never have seen the benefits of conscious living.

I hope you, too, have started to feel grateful for the way difficult periods in your life are now finally bearing fruit. In any case, I really think you deserve a nice *treat!* Allow yourself a celebration and pat yourself on the back. You are now officially halfway through our journey together. *Well done!*

Over the next six months/weeks, you will begin to use the tools you've learned through the previous journey. The chance that you'll be able to finally materialise your dream is getting more realistic.

You might feel that I'm repeating myself, and you are right, I do. However, it is through repetition that we learn.

—That's it for now.

NEXT TIME:

- How can we improve our financial situations?
- How can we improve our health?
- How can we attract the right people into our lives?

SEVENTH JOURNEY TOGETHER

WHAT HAVE YOU DISCOVERED SO FAR?

You know:

- Your dream and what kind of personality you have
- What direction you are taking your life
- Why life needs to suck in between
- How to soothe yourself
- How to practise gratitude daily
- How to add things to your daily life that make you happy
- How to do your daily meditation practice
- How to make important decisions
- How to deal with anxiety and depression
- How to look at suicide and death
- What your right path is

- Why diversity is so important
- What causes the extreme weather

If you need to, go back and revisit the previous assignments. ☺

FINANCIAL SITUATION

Working very, very hard is usually not the answer. You might create a better financial situation, but you won't feel better having it if what you do feels hard. So how can you create a good financial situation for yourself and still feel good?

Most of us believe that the world's resources are limited and have forgotten that we create everything we want through our thoughts. If we focus on the resources being limited, we only see the limitations.

By following your passion instead of only being guided by money and good finances, you will shift your focus towards what feels good and gives you pleasure. In addition, if you have faith in yourself and your own creativity, you will automatically be sucked into the Vortex, where all the goods you can imagine are created.

By keeping your feelings up in joy, inspiration and enthusiasm as often as you can, the likelihood is great that you will also be able to materialise the goods of your dream into your physical existence.

In fact, your job is only to allow your dreams to have free flow so that the dreams do not constantly meet closed doors. If you keep your feelings deep down in the low vibrations, you will not be able to "hear when your dream knocks on the door."

In other words, by being completely down in the basement of your emotional life, you will not be able to listen to the impulses and inspirations flowing from within because you are focusing your attention on all the problems in your life. If you are down in the basement, you are unlikely to meet the right people, go to the right places or make the decisions that can be crucial for fulfilling your dreams.

Your attitude towards having plenty and living a good and prosperous life might also prevent you from living a lifestyle of abundance.

If you talk disparagingly about your rich neighbour, family member or friend, you are not allowing abundance and good fortune to flow freely to yourself.

Many of us remember the Bible story about the rich man who is as likely to enter Paradise as a camel is to pass through the eye of a needle. Being critical of rich people has, for a long time, been an accepted attitude among Christians, but also among other people.

As everywhere else in life, the Law of Attraction is also at work when it comes to attracting abundance. By focusing on your own lack of money or thinking that having plenty of money is undesirable, you attract more feelings of lacking money and draw more rich people into your daily view, making you feel the lack even more.

Our behaviour towards rich people might also stem from jealousy. Being jealous creates low energy, as does having a judgemental attitude. If you keep your feelings at the low part of the scale of emotions, you'll just create more situations that add to the low energies.

The opposite happens if you choose to keep yourself at the top of the scale of emotions. If you feel happy for the people who have plenty and have an attitude that abundance would be welcome in your life too, you are vibrating at a station where abundance is created.

The trick is that you need to **allow** the abundance to flow your way. If you lose hope because money is short when you really need it, you immediately close the door on abundance. Remembering Abraham's fourth and fifth steps is the key: stay in the high vibrations but forgive yourself when you drop. That way you will stay in the Vortex longer; however, you need to be patient and focused.

As you can see, it's not so much what we **do** that leads us to fulfil our wishes. The most important thing is to become aware of how we choose to **think and feel**. Everything we have asked for in our physical existence is already waiting for us at the upper part of the scale of emotions. Inside the Vortex, the Source starts working on our desires as soon as we've launched them. It's similar to when we plant a seed: we need to be patient, watering and caring for the seed until it can bear fruit. The same goes for our desire.

By moving yourself up the scale of emotions to the Vortex, where all abundance is waiting for you, you can start showing gratitude for any gift you receive like a new day, a smile, or a bird's twittering. In this way you train yourself to feel grateful, which will help you reach the Vortex and the good feelings at the top of the scale of emotions.

Many of us find it difficult to receive. We might feel indebted to the giver or not able to appreciate the gift because it's not to our liking, or we may have expected more. With this attitude, we destroy our opportunity to receive and we slide down the scale of emotions. Even if you are not yet able to see the proof of your desires, by keeping your feelings of expectancy, faith and hope, you'll slowly open the door to abundance and let all the good stuff pour in. Keeping yourself at the top part of the scale all the time isn't possible, however, because contrast is needed to put forward new longings and desires for better living conditions to ensure more change and growth in the world.

Furthermore, we all need to be challenged. Life would soon become boring if we could just sit on our couches and order from the top shelf without having to do anything to get our wishes down from the shelf. It would be like playing a game where we hit the finish line at the first roll of the dice.

Meditating, making a list of things to be grateful for, putting your focus on the good stuff in your life and choosing to do things that make you happy are examples of different ways to again open the door to the Vortex.

When you wake up in the morning, you can choose to think or meditate yourself into knowing that everything is working out for you and that there's no reason to worry. By staying in this good-feeling place as long as possible during your day, you make sure to put yourself in a receptive mood that will take you up to the high vibrations, where good stuff, people and situations can enter your life. You can also spend time visualising and enjoying your dream long before it has become reality.

As you can see, receiving abundance works pretty much the same way as raising children. "Be happy, patient and grateful, and you'll have your present."

By consciously using your tools, you'll finally manage to reach the highest vibrations of passion, love and joy. Even if you can't stay here for very long, it's still worth reaching for, as being at the top of your vibrations is a lot like "coming home," where everything you need is taken care of.

However, if you're in the habit of feeling poor as soon as your pocket is empty, you unconsciously let yourself slide down to the lower vibrations.

If you are impatient and want everything right now and don't have time to wait until you see that your financial situation can handle a purchase, you can easily become a victim of expensive credit. Expensive credit will, in the end, make you feel trapped and the feeling of constraint will quickly drag you down into the basement, where you feel fear, depression and powerlessness.

Putting money aside will ensure peace of mind, which is necessary in order to keep our vibrations up. Remember, if your focus is on lack, you'll just receive more lack; if your focus is on gratitude, you'll receive more to be grateful for.

By making sure you always have some money put aside, you create an opportunity to feel good no matter how little your abundance is. At the same time, you are giving yourself the opportunity to keep yourself in the vibrations of receiving.

Should you experience the loss of your home, business or empire due to external causes such as disasters or major economic changes in society, Abraham asks you not to despair, but rather to focus on rebuilding. If you have built it before, you will manage to build it again. Life is a process where the goal is not to be done, but to continually find improvements and new solutions. This makes me think of the artist who makes his masterpiece in ice or in the sand on the beach. Everything we build is perishable. If we manage to focus on the joy of creation and let go of the fear that what we create will be lost, we will feel much freer. The challenge is that such an attitude towards life requires a very strong consciousness.

ASSIGNMENT 19

Write down what you think is stopping you from receiving the good stuff in life. What habits can you change that keep you in the low vibrations?

My Turn

What things have stopped me from receiving

Since I was very young, I have felt really sad seeing the big differences between people and I had a strong wish that resources should be equally distributed. When I moved to Africa, these feelings got even stronger. I literally felt sick seeing the long line of poor people outside our gate asking for jobs or some alms.

With both my husband and I working for the UN and having everything we could ask for (unlike the people outside our door, who hardly had what they needed to survive), I began to feel rage towards the Source. I couldn't understand how a creator could see this unfairness and do nothing. Then, returning to Norway and taking on a job that I needed to be able to renovate my rundown house, I experienced the feeling of being poor myself.

The money I had left was hardly enough to cover my electricity bill. At one point, my money concerns were so bad that I didn't want to open the mailbox, fearing it would contain more bills. And, of course, it did. The more fearful I became, the more problems I encountered. In the end, I was so tired of my house and my life being ill that I stopped caring about anything at all and, from there, my situation started slowly but surely to turn. At that stage, I was completely down in the basement of my emotional scale and the only direction I could move was upwards.

Many years later, I understood that it would help nobody if I gave away all my belongings to the poor. It would be, as Abraham says, like me taking on an illness for the sake of making somebody else healthy. Helping poor people believe that they, too, can create the lives they want through expecting good things to come to them and giving them faith in their own creation are much better alternatives to giving our stuff away.

Today, I understand why some people are poor and some people are rich. First of all, we chose to be born into different societies and families because we wanted different challenges. Some choose tougher challenges than others. Even being pretty, healthy and rich can have its challenges. However, these challenges are on a completely different level compared to those who choose disease, malformation and poverty.

Becoming used to having little, we are not prone to expecting much more from our lives. Many poor people I know live good lives as long as their neighbours are in the same situation. The difficulties start when a neighbour gets money or a rich guy moves in to their neighbourhood. Instead of being jealous, the poor people could use the neighbour's new lifestyle as proof that it is possible to lift themselves out of poverty. Through faith and knowledge of how thoughts attract, the poor people will also be able to create a better life.

Even the rich, pretty and healthy may need this insight, as it is not what we can touch that makes us happy. If we are wealthy but lack the ability to be kind, patient and grateful, we have nothing of real value. Our heavy thoughts will keep us away from the happiness, love and freedom that we only find on the high vibrating station and we will then feel emotionally poor.

I still give alms and I still do volunteer work, but I have begun to expect more in return for the hours that I'm spending trying to make this world evolve. Thinking along these lines, I decided to make money from what I do and not work for free so often. A few years ago, I would have struggled with a thought like this, as I would have thought that I had enough money. Now, on the other hand, I have finally started to feel that I'm worth the recognition a good income will give me.

If we don't have an expectation, or we think it's wrong to earn money, or we are so poor that we don't believe it's even possible to attract abundance because we've never seen anybody in our situation being able to change their life, it's not likely that we will see much change.

To attract anything, we need to first ask and then believe that, in time, our wish will be granted. And while we wait, we can focus on the good things in our lives at the moment, even if the only good thing is that we are still breathing. It can sound incredibly hard, but actually, it's only a choice of thought. Throughout history, very many people have raised themselves from two empty hands. "**When others can do that, we can do it too.**" ☺

Having expectations of other people and situations that you don't control is completely different from having expectations of what you yourself believe you can master and create. If you have no expectation of yourself and your own inner power, you will not visualise and dream of achieving anything in your life, and the probability that you will then make major changes is dramatically reduced.

Some people are very ill or have physical or mental challenges that make them dependent on other people. However, we cannot write off these people's positive impact on themselves and the people around them.

One of the people who has inspired me most through my own depressive times was paralysed from the neck down. Despite needing help with everything, she found great pleasure in reading books and listening to the radio. She also enjoyed conversations where we discussed the meaning of life.

Some days she was depressed, but mostly she was happy and pleased with her life. One day, as we were talking, she said, "For many years, I used my time thinking about how my life would have been if I was healthy. I also asked myself what I had done wrong to get paralysed. But nothing good came out of these thoughts. Now I have chosen to focus on how lucky I am that I can live my life through the books and the radio. All I have to do is choose books and programs that make me happy, and then life is actually not too bad."

Your Turn

If you find yourself in need of more abundance, this is a great exercise to focus on. You will have to examine your thoughts and feelings about money to clear all your doubts and fears about receiving abundance. At the same time, it is important to be aware of how you spend your money and what you want to achieve.

If you have substantial and expensive debt and feel trapped, get help to pay off your debt as quickly as possible. Then make a plan for saving. At the same time, scrutinise how you shop. What do you really need? What is being thrown away or left unused when it comes to food, clothing, shoes or equipment? Also, look at habits that initially cost little but are expensive in the long run, such as café food and drinks. Stop regular expenses that you don't use, such as memberships to groups or services you no longer attend, and go through insurance policies and loans and see if you can get them cheaper.

By getting an overview of how much money you have available per month after all fixed expenses are paid, you can either withdraw a quarter of the remaining amount in cash every week or transfer the amount to a separate account to avoid exceeding your budget. Finally, establish a savings account. When done, you can breathe out with relief! You will now feel more conscious, safe and free and, with this highly vibrating positive feeling, you will be able to direct your life in a good financial direction much more easily.

> **MANTRA:** Through conscious thoughts, patience and a thoughtful way to spend, my money seed will start to grow.

HEALTH

There are so many health recipes out there contradicting each other about how we can best keep healthy, and I don't want to add to this confusion. Everything in life has to do with what we believe in, so if you believe and also see results from your health treatment, please don't change anything. However, if you haven't found any relief to your health issues, you might find this reading interesting.

The only thing that's important is that you find relief; how you find it isn't important. This, of course, assumes that you don't harm your environment or anybody around you during the process of getting your treatment.

The placebo effect is the best cure that ever existed, and the reason why it has been shown to be so effective is that it's our thoughts that make us ill and it's our thoughts that make us healthy. When we believe in a treatment, we start to expect results and, as it gives us faith and hope, our vibrations heighten and the door to the Vortex opens. And when the door to the Vortex opens, we can't feel pain.

Everything in existence is made of energy, including our cells. When we are fearful, we stop the energy flow to our cells and our immune system stops operating properly. This way, we unconsciously create illness. We are our own physicians and executioners in the way we choose to think. Through our thoughts and feelings, we attract both health and sickness. We even attract situations and people into our lives that can heal or destroy us. Whatever happens to us is all of our own making, Abraham explains.

You might think it's irritating that you now have nobody to blame, but, on the other hand, this knowledge gives you the power to handle everything yourself just through the way you choose to think. However, in today's society, few of us have come so far that we believe our thoughts can heal us without any form of medicine. Therefore, most of us will need treatment from outside our thoughts. But the treatment you choose won't matter as much as your belief in the medicine's healing effect.

Nevertheless, in your eagerness for good health you must not forget that most of us go in and out of balance in terms of illness and health and it's quite natural to get sick as a response to our imbalanced thoughts. However, pain and sickness are only a result of you choosing to not listen to the guidance of your inner being.

When you are sick and feel pain, depending on how sick you are of course, sleep and entertainment are two good ways to get your mind away from the pain and hook up with your inner being. Watching a fun program on TV, reading a good book or talking to someone who makes you laugh are great aids, since laughter and good thoughts help us to shift our focus away from sickness, fear and depression and enable us to feel pleasure.

In this way, you will again open the energy flow to your cells so that the immune system can get the chance to heal you.

If you look into which food to eat and which exercises to do, the only recommendations Abraham Hicks gives are to drink plenty of water, to eat food as free from additives as possible, and that all exercises involving conscious breathing are good for us. Otherwise, Abraham doesn't warn against any habits we have, as he says our thinking of things as being bad for us makes them even worse.

By taking responsibility for your own life in the way you think and feel, you'll automatically be guided to the medication, food and lifestyle that suit you.

What's healthy and good for some is not necessarily healthy and good for all, though. The Maasai in Tanzania and Kenya have lived mainly on blood and milk for centuries, without getting sicker, for that reason. Abraham says that using energy to worry that we do not eat the "right" food can be more harmful than eating junk food, if we manage to do this with a good conscience and happy thoughts. The reason for this is that our thoughts and feelings are much, much more important to our health than the food we feed our body. Abraham also says that, to enable your body to detox and keep your cells healthy, 90% of all fluid intake needs to be water. However, if you make this into a problem on the days you don't drink as much water, your negative thoughts are more harmful for your body than less water intake.

If you believe that babies can't be responsible for their own sickness because they don't have a language or thoughts of their own, then you have forgotten that a baby is usually an old soul that has chosen to enter a new body for a new physical experience. And all souls, old and new, are given feelings as their guiding system and will be able to make their own choices about health and sickness.

Some, on the other hand, have deliberately chosen to acquire new knowledge through illness. This could either be through the challenge of healing oneself or through the challenge of learning to live with the pain that disease brings.

As in most other areas of life, however, we can take on challenges that are too big and thereby feel forced to throw in the towel. Some choose, either deliberately or unconsciously, to withdraw from their lives. The unconscious way of withdrawing from our physical form is through accident, cardiac arrest or illness.

ASSIGNMENT 20

If you have a health issue, write down the thoughts you believe your problem stems from. Now write down examples of new thoughts that can help improve your health.

If you believe in your medication and your own way of life, do not seek to make any changes. Your belief and your positive attitude towards life will finally make you feel better.

My Turn

Thoughts That My Health Issues Stem From

Looking back at the time when I got diabetes and became depressed, I was so stressed and so frustrated over life that it's no wonder I became ill. The way I chose to handle my life was far from optimal. Instead of finding solutions, I just added fire to the problems and didn't stop until I was unable to stand on my own two feet.

This kind of behaviour is a result of an imbalanced solar plexus. The solar plexus is the third energy centre, located in the region below the ribcage and the area where our pancreas is located and insulin is produced. The solar plexus helps to balance our energy, makes us confident and independent, and gives us willpower.

In the way I chose to think, I damaged this energy centre, and the result was a broken pancreas and no energy whatsoever. Choosing to meditate and give rest to my unhealthy thoughts was the first way to get myself back on track. Choosing to do things I loved to do, such as reading and writing, was the next. However, it was not until I understood that I could create the life I wanted just through my own thoughts and feelings that my life really changed for the better.

I now know how to monitor my thoughts by being conscious of how I feel, and I have made "good feelings" my top priority. If I feel bad, I don't use time and energy thinking too much about why I feel this way, as it will just take me further down. Instead, I try to see the situation differently or take a nap, meditate or find something to distract me from my unproductive thoughts. If I can't manage to change my feelings today, I know that tomorrow holds a new fresh start for good thoughts and feelings.

In order for tomorrow to be good, it requires me to be conscious when I go to bed. It also requires me to be aware the next morning and to start the new day in a positive and conscious manner. By making a gratitude list before I fall asleep and by trying to see my situation with new eyes before I go to bed, I significantly increase my chance of being awarded new opportunities. If I fall asleep in frustration, I often wake up with frustration, and there is a high likelihood that I will bring my heavy thoughts into the new day.

I have not been able to heal my diabetes to the extent that I no longer need insulin injections, as I guess my beliefs are too influenced by the society I've grown up in. Nobody I know believes it's possible to awaken a dead pancreas, at least not my doctors.

Anyway, today my diabetes doesn't affect me much except for the need my body has for insulin injections, and sometimes I get insulin shock by giving myself too much, but I've become used to keeping carbohydrates with me. As long as I'm able to monitor my energy level through balanced blood sugar, calmness and good feelings, I can now live the life I always dreamed of.

Your Turn

If you have a health issue, write down the thoughts you believe your problem stems from. Now write down examples of new thoughts that can help improve your health.

You can still do this assignment even if you have no health issues; being conscious of your own well-being and energy level will allow you to discover what is needed to heighten it even further.

> **MANTRA:** It's not what happens to me but how I react to it that matters.

ATTRACTING A PARTNER

I guess you have discovered by now that whatever you want to bring into your life has everything to do with the way you choose to think and feel.

If you don't monitor your thoughts and instead allow yourself to vibrate on the lowest parts of the scale of emotions, you'll be sure to attract people who also vibrate at this level.

If you like to surround yourself with positive, happy, passionate and loving people, you will need to speed up your energy and vibrate where these people are located.

We seldom find that a passionate, happy person is attracted to a depressed, negative one, but, if so, the relationship will not be a happy one. This is also the reason why we see so many divorces, as it's very hard to live with a person who doesn't vibrate on our own energy level.

There might not be anything wrong with the person we once chose to live with, it's just that the attraction disappears as soon as we start vibrating on different channels. Finding a way back to the same channel might be the solution, but to put ourselves down in the low vibrations is not a good choice.

Forcing your partner to come up to your station will not work either, as everyone is responsible for their own vibrations. Keeping your vibrations up despite your partner's mood is the only way you can create change. By being a good example, seeing your partner in the way the Source does, you might create space in which your partner can feel their own inner guiding system and choose to heighten their vibrations.

To attract the love of your dreams, the same rules also apply here. If you are able to expect, as well as have faith and hope, that one day your dream partner will show up, then your feelings are already in the top part of the scale of emotions, which implies that you are also able to thrive without the materialisation of your dream. In this case, as soon as you are a match to your dream partner's energy level, the prince or princess will have to emerge.

In fact, there is no point in spending time and effort looking for him or her. You will automatically attract your dream partner the day you are a match. All you need to do is follow your impulses and enjoy the idea that your dream partner is just waiting for you to get ready.

If you feel that your life is almost not worth living without your dream partner, then you will attract a partner with a personality that reinforces your feeling of longing. Your focus is then on the lack of what you want, and not on expectation, joy, faith and hope that your dream will be fulfilled the day you are ready for such a relationship.

In other words, you will not be able to attract people who operate high on the scale of emotions if you operate on a lower vibrating channel. This does not mean, however, that your dream partner needs to be completely like you for you to attract each other, only that your feelings vibrate at the same frequency.

If we vibrate on the same channel, we may fit together like a hand in a glove. We may be different but compatible, as the energy level we both vibrate on will ensure we take advantage of any inequalities. We will make the inequalities our strength or our weakness, depending on whether we're talking about high or low vibration channels.

If both people in a relationship have feelings that are mainly down the scale, where we find fear, hatred and low self-worth, and therefore often operate at the lowest-vibrating frequencies, they will fit together as a hand in a glove but in a negative way, similar to relationships that are characterised by an attacker and a victim, a dominant and a submissive person, or one who is narcissistic and one who is self-effacing.

If both vibrate on the same high-frequency channel, they have complementarity where, for instance, one is calm and the other is outgoing, one is practical and the other is theoretical, or one is creative and the other is structured.

In order to attract the people you want into your life, it's advisable to be aware of which channel you most often vibrate at and change frequency if you see that you operate in the low vibrations. You can do this by remembering to use your tools.

ASSIGNMENT 21

First, describe the qualities of the person you want to attract. Then find the level on the scale of emotions where this person vibrates. Be honest with yourself and see where on the scale of emotions you usually keep yourself. Finally, use your thoughts to adjust yourself to the channel where your choice of person vibrates and try to stay there as often as you can.

Remember: You can't do anything wrong no matter what you do, as we all need imbalance. Each of us attracts people and situations that we don't like, but we decide whether these experiences can be used for learning or for blame. If you choose blame, the feeling of stagnation and pain can be the result.

My Turn

How I Found My Prince

When we were renovating our house in Norway, I was so angry with my husband that, if he hadn't been so far away, working in Africa, I would have wrung his neck. He had no understanding of what it was like to live inside a renovation project with two children, and he always complained about the choices I made, not taking the time to make the decisions together with me.

Later, when he moved back home, I had no energy left to wring his neck and our life together became a real challenge. During that time, I started dreaming of a prince who would come and rescue me from my sad life, and I made a list of qualities that I wanted this prince of mine to have. It was a long list of superlatives that I, at that time, was not even close to matching. I still have my journal in which I made the list, and it's really interesting to see that this prince is now part of my life.

It took many years for me to change my thoughts to come up to the vibrating level of the prince I had imagined. Today, I'm so happy that I'm still sharing my life with the husband I married, as he's now the prince of my dreams, the same one I dreamed of through the heaviest years of disease and depression. Checking the list after so many years, I discovered that my husband scored nine of the thirteen superlatives I had on the list describing my dream prince.

The interesting thing about this discovery is that my husband has not changed significantly. Instead, the change has mostly occurred in me. When I previously chose to focus on the four things I didn't like about my husband's personality, only the characteristics I disliked became visible to me, and thus I was unable to see or experience all the qualities that I liked.

> Everyone has a "shadow side" and features that have potential for improvement, and we are all most concerned about ourselves. We can try to argue that we are more concerned about others' well-being than our own, but if we were sincerely more concerned with the happiness of others, we would easily become self-effacing and doormats for others.

The community, our parents, school and our religions want us to feel bad if we choose our own happiness over others. That's how it has been since times immemorial. And why is it still like that? By giving people who we want to obey us a bad conscience, we believe that they will be easier to control. However, we came to this world to focus on our own growth and development and, in order to manage this focus, we must follow our own happiness, dreams and wishes for life.

> If you believe you can transfer responsibility to other people to make you happy when you are basically not happy with yourself, then you have not yet understood how life works. Being happy is only your own responsibility, because being happy lies in your own thoughts and no other people can control your thoughts and feelings. When you choose to wait for circumstances or people around you to behave exactly as you wish before you choose to feel happy, you will not experience many moments of happiness. However, if you choose to be happy regardless of your surroundings by keeping the focus on the things that actually work and that are good and beautiful, you will attract more and more people, things and situations to be happy about.
>
> Should you choose to live your life together with another person, it may be a good idea to look closely at your partner's imbalanced sides and assess whether you can manage to live with this imbalance as well. It's very difficult to change other people. Should you manage to change yourself, it must, as previously discussed, come from a deep personal desire for change.

Having said that, we're all changing and some people change faster than others. This can make a promise of eternal faithfulness very difficult to keep, especially if your partner develops in a negative direction. Abraham says that, instead of giving wedding vows, we could agree to live together and see how things evolve. This is because wedding vows may be impossible to keep if your partner tries to prevent you in your own development or does not have an interest in growing and developing him or herself.

Your Turn

Make a list of the qualities of the person you want to attract. Check if you have these qualities yourself. If not, try to raise your own vibrations to the station where your dream partner vibrates.

This is an assignment that is nice to do, as it can be great fun to go back to after you've found your prince or princess or, as in my case, reinvented your prince. However, it's important to find a balance where you try to keep yourself up in the high vibrations, as it's quite natural to slip down the scale of emotions.

If you then blame yourself or become disappointed that you are not "perfect" (which none of us are or are meant to be), it will eventually be impossible to reach the good feelings, and you'll then achieve the opposite of what you want.

In other words: in order to reach the high vibrations, you must be kind and good to yourself and accept that you frequently fail. If you do that, you won't focus on other people's mistakes either; you'll become more accepting and understanding of the fact that we all fail and get out of balance. The trick is thus: allow yourself to fail, try to learn from it and soothe yourself up the scale of emotions again ... and again ... and again ... and again ... And at the same time, know that the mistakes you make will bring you, maybe not a big, but at least a small step forward.

> **MANTRA:** I attract people who fit me like a hand in a glove.

—That's it for now.

NEXT TIME:

- How to handle difficult people
- When children are difficult
- How to relax when life is stressful

EIGHTH JOURNEY TOGETHER

DIFFICULT PEOPLE

If you get annoyed by people, that's a good sign that you have slid down into the lower vibrations on the scale of emotions. If not, you wouldn't notice or care about how *terribly* difficult some people can sometimes be!

To be sure not to attract those horrible, annoying people, you can keep calm and know that they actually can't harm you as long as you don't let them annoy you. Easier said than done? Yeah, I know it's incredibly difficult, especially when you are taken by surprise.

If you can't escape an interaction with a "horrible" person, but you have some warning, you can train yourself to see this person through the eyes of the Source, as the Source loves us all, even if we haven't figured out how to love ourselves and our world.

If that doesn't work, you can look at this person as somebody who has no influence on your life – like somebody you observe on the street. With some practice, it will work; however, it might take some time.

ASSIGNMENT 22

If you have a difficult person in your life, think through how you can change your view of this person or how you can focus on their good behaviour.

My Turn

My "horrible," difficult, annoying person is now long-dead, and it's very strange to discover that I really miss her. She was a family member and somebody very hard to escape. I feel her on my shoulder while I'm sitting writing about her; she's laughing, as if it was all a big joke.

For more than twenty years, I believed that it was impossible to encounter a worse person. She was directly mean to me, and if there's anyone in this life who I could say that I hated, it was this woman. The strange thing was that sometimes I really liked her, but then she suddenly screamed at me for no reason at all, taking me off guard almost every time, and I had no way of preparing myself.

I'm not sure what happened, but when this woman got old and a bit senile and needed my help, she started to like me. I went to visit her often, discovering that I really enjoyed the time I spent with her. She was very knowledgeable, and she could also be funny. However, if she didn't like somebody, she would still bark like a mad dog, scaring the crap out of people.

Looking back, I wish I'd had the knowledge I have today, as this woman would have been the perfect person to train myself with. If I could have handled her outbursts without quaking, I'm sure I would have been able to handle any difficult person.

Don Miguel Ruiz wrote the book *The Four Agreements*. One of these agreements is not to take anything personally. I use this advice in my daily life today.

When people are misbehaving or say ugly words to me, I now understand that it is, in most cases, because they don't feel good about themselves, as they are disconnected and not in touch with their inner beings. We can all get angry with others and try to find fault in our fellow human beings. Often the real problem is that we are tired, annoyed or angry with ourselves. If you can avoid taking things personally, it helps both you and those who let their frustration out on others. If we take what is being said personally, we will trigger an avalanche of bad situations that will not benefit anyone.

The exercise mentioned below is a good example of how, when we focus on one aspect of a situation, we can completely ignore other aspects of the same situation. Although the website does not look at human relations, it still illustrates that, if we focus on the negative aspects of a fellow human being, that will be all we see. On the other hand, if we decide to fully focus on the good things, it is most likely that this is what we will notice. This means that we will see what we focus on.

If you would like, you can try this for yourself by doing the experiment. You'll find it on my website: **https://www.a-life-worth-living.org/ feel-good-links/inspiration/**. (Watch the monkey business illusion.)

Your Turn

Most people have somebody in their life who they find difficult. It might be a teacher, a boss, a family member, a colleague, a schoolmate or somebody else who isn't easy to get away from.

You can train yourself to deal with your difficult person to keep them from hurting you anymore. If you keep letting them scare or annoy you, you'll just allow your energy level to drop. Sometimes it's better to try to let them like you despite their behaviour not being acceptable, as trying to make someone change is extremely difficult and not your job. Your job is to keep yourself as happy as possible.

It's worthwhile to find a technique that works for you. In order to live your dream, you need to make sure your vibrations are on top – not all of the time, but as much of the time as possible. Should your difficult person also abuse you physically, your best choice is to get help and move yourself out of their way. However, in order to prevent a new abuser from entering your life, it is important to forgive and move your focus towards your future dream. A negative focus will just prevent you from reaching the high vibrations where you can find your dream of a good future.

> **MANTRA:** If I stay up with the high vibrations, nobody can harm me against my will.

WHEN CHILDREN ARE DIFFICULT

If you're a parent, you'll often experience children being difficult. Feeling the responsibility of raising your child towards good behaviour and a happy life can be a challenge.

As we've discussed before, our feelings are our guiding system that tells us when our thoughts correlate with our inner being and the Source. When we deviate from our happy journey down the river, we shut down the energy flow between us and the Source. This makes us feel worse.

When you, as a parent, get in the way of your child connecting with their own guiding system by either comforting or scolding the child, it makes it harder for the child to connect with their own emotions. This is why it's usually better to give the child some space to figure out how to turn their emotions and heighten their vibrations on their own without your interaction.

If you are conscious and notice that the child's mood is going downhill, you can divert the child's attention away from bad thoughts. If, on the other hand, you are too late, there is not much you can do until the child has hit rock bottom.

By focusing on the child's bad behaviour or feeling sorry for the child and starting to comfort unnecessarily, you prevent the child from soothing themselves up the scale of emotions. If you don't see the importance of keeping yourself calm, this can make the child dependent on always gaining attention or comfort outside of themself. This response pattern can eventually follow the child all the way up to adulthood and can cause a lot of unnecessary drama, as it is through drama that this person will try to force comfort or attention from their surroundings.

However, when the child is happy, that's the time to cuddle and praise the child and give them as much attention as possible. This way, the child will long for the good times and make their downtime as short as possible, as there are no good feelings or attention to attract them to the lower vibrations.

Your task is to be as good a role model as possible by showing the child how they can choose to handle difficult situations a little better. But doing this when the child is at full speed downhill won't work. By waiting for the emotions to calm down, you will have a much better opportunity to guide the child towards good thoughts and a good life.

ASSIGNMENT 23

When your child (if you have one) is being difficult, try not to give him or her attention, but rather go about your life as normal. It is much better to talk to the child about what happened at a later time, when you are both happy and satisfied. Then write down your observations in your workbook.

My Turn

When I was being difficult as a child, I remember that my mother told me to go into my room and not come back until I felt happy again. I must have been a very easy child because I did as she told me and soon came out of my room feeling much better.

When I had children of my own, looking back to my own childhood, I thought my mother's behaviour towards me when I was upset was cold compared to that of my friends' parents, who would cuddle them and try to do whatever it took to make their children feel happy again.

Forgetting what an easy, happy child I once was, I decided to do everything in my power to keep my children happy. So, when they cried or became upset, I would sit "forever" trying to figure out the reason for their behaviour, and often I worried when it seemed like nothing could comfort them.

After a while, with lots of worries, my energy level dropped and I was not able to keep myself up to speed with all the attention my children would need. If they then threw a tantrum, I would snap at them, making them very confused, as they would think this was the time for their cuddle.

By teaching our children that attention and love are the response to low vibrations, we totally misguide them, making them depend on other people to take them up to the higher vibrations.

Fortunately, as time goes by and their parents are out of the way, children usually figure out how to connect with their own guiding systems. However, it would save us all a lot of energy if we knew earlier in life how to take ourselves up to the happy vibrations by knowing how to connect with our own emotions without the confusion and worries from our parents.

Your Turn

If you don't have children of your own, you can practise when you are around other people's children.

> **MANTRA:** My children have their own guiding system that will take them up to the high vibrations. My task is to be as good a role model as possible.

STRESS

As far as I believe, we were all Source energy before taking on a body to go for a new ride and help the universe expand.

Even if you are not consciously aware of it, all your body cells communicate directly with the Source. However, as Abraham explains, when you keep thinking thoughts that do not correspond with your inner being, you block the communication between your cells and the Source and, in this way, you unconsciously create stress and pain in your body.

Stress is not directly correlated to how much you have to do; instead, it has everything to do with how you think and feel about your life and what you do. If you think you are not good enough, if you have a need to control other people or your surroundings, if you don't like what you are doing, if you find your life overwhelming, and if your thoughts contradict each other, that's when you feel stress.

When you stress, you hold your cork under the water. Letting go of the cork is the only thing that you need to do. In other words, choosing better-feeling thoughts is the solution. It will help if you can become conscious of what it is that makes you stressed by asking yourself questions, but if you go too deep into asking why, you just put focus on the problem, not the solution.

Is there a better way of looking at my situation? This is a great question. It also helps if you are able to stop what you are doing and not start again until you are able to feel like doing it. Using meditation, gratitude and "This will also pass" or "Everything is working out for me" statements are all good tools to get yourself up to the high vibrations.

After unblocking your energy, you can work almost nonstop except for the hours when you need to sleep and eat. Doing what you do because you like it will not drain you but rather fill you with energy, and you will also perform much better.

Knowing that you'll never get it done and that you can't get it wrong, there is no reason to get stressed about anything, not even over exams or contests, as failing is part of your learning process. During eternity, you'll have plenty of new chances to get it right. However, for some of us it feels important to get our exam right the first time.

Learning anything is much easier when we can see the value of learning the skills, though. Forcing yourself to do something that seems useless you push your cork underwater. It is much more fruitful to feel inspired, even if you are not doing anything, until your vibrations are on top. This way, you will save yourself a lot of time and energy!

By unblocking your energy, you connect yourself automatically with the infinite intelligence that is the Source. Being connected, you have access to all knowledge and you'll know the right time to say or do anything. This is also how you make sure you put your seeds of inspiration in fertile soil.

Connecting to your inner knowledge is, however, impossible when you block out the Source from your life by forcing things. This is why a relaxed attitude towards life often takes us much further on our journeys and – the best part – with this attitude, the ride will feel much more fun.

Working really, really hard can also take us far. The drawback is that it's exhausting and no fun at all.

Patience and giving myself more time are two good tricks that have helped me relax. A few years back, I was an impatient soul who hated spending unnecessary time waiting. If I was stuck in a traffic jam and it looked like I was going to arrive at my appointments late, I would stress my whole body into tension. Choosing to have plenty of time and giving myself the opportunity to relax and enjoy my journey has helped me to lower my shoulders and feel good in most situations.

ASSIGNMENT 24

When you feel stressed, write down how you can look at your life differently and what changes you can make.

My Turn

During my house-renovating project, I totally freaked out, as forcing things didn't work.

Coming home during winter after eight years in Africa, alone with two children, could be a challenge in itself. But seeing our old house standing on metal stilts with no basement and not being able to enter the front door was really a shock.

Outside on a stormy winter night with the kids and luggage around my legs, my first thought was, "This can't be true. Why didn't anyone warn me about this?" The plan had been to come home to a finished basement apartment and live there while the rest of the house was being renovated.

Then I inhaled a couple of deep, icy breaths, trying to get an overview of the situation. Finally, I thought that, if I had survived Africa, I could survive this, too – that is, if I could just find a way to enter the house! No worries. My two sons had already found a way to the kitchen door via a wooden plank that crossed over the deep ditch surrounding the house.

Entering the house, it was freezing cold, and the beds were smelly. It was so cold inside that there was no chance of sleeping for the first two nights. Later, we were told that the builders had encountered a problem in the ground under the house and had left it without telling us, not even leaving any heaters on.

Without a water heater or washing machine, we washed our bedsheets in the kitchen sink and wrung them out in the snow outside, with my two boys at one end of the sheets and me at the other. At first, I was proud of my sons and myself for managing to find solutions to one problem at a time. We were now able to sleep, as the mattresses had dried out. We had also managed to clean our sheets and dry them by hanging them in front of the red-glowing wood stove in the living room.

It was also nice to discover that my children were happy coming back to Norway and that they very much looked forward to experiencing a real winter. The challenge, though, was to find the money to buy all the equipment they needed, as the building problem meant our renovating costs had doubled – and, a few months later, they tripled.

In spite of the sky-high unemployment rate in Norway at that time, I was still determined to find a job. I was on my knees begging for work and, when I finally did get a job, I was so, so happy. As it was holiday season, I started the job by covering for two colleagues who were on vacation. Sitting glued to the phone and the computer the whole day and not having a headset, I developed a problem in my shoulder that kept me awake most of the night and, slowly but surely, I started to stress out.

When a colleague asked me to come to town with her on a Friday night, I declined, explaining about the huge pile of unfinished work I had on my desk and how tired I was.

My colleague just chuckled, as if I had told her a funny story. Then she became serious. "You should know by now that you'll never be finished. Every week there will be new piles of work, and on and on it goes. Relax, Nina," she said, "or you're not going to cope with the pressure." But I was too tired and stressed to relax.

There was no way I could manage to sleep after getting restless legs in addition to the shoulder pain and, on top of that, a headache from always thinking about where we would get the money to finish the house. When the summer came, with bright short nights and children who did not want to go to bed, I finally collapsed during a lunch break at work and was transported to the hospital in an ambulance. Here I was diagnosed with diabetes. The rest of the story you already know. The point is, how could I have done this differently?

First of all, I could have asked my parents to help me out and not tried to handle everything by myself. I could have asked my boss for a headset much earlier. I could have said no to my children and husband when they demanded too much of me. In other words, I could have been much more selfish and taken better care of myself.

Secondly, I could have kept my thoughts focused, relaxing in the knowledge that this situation would also pass and that everything would work out for me as long as I stayed connected to the Source. Even if I block out the Source, things will always work out for me, as my pain will make sure I hook up with the Source again, with or without my body.

Because I didn't know the importance of monitoring my feelings and my energy level, I got frustrated, more and more angry, and, later, depressed about my situation. I had blocked my connection to the Source, and my pain became intolerable. In addition, I had managed to block the energy flow to my solar plexus to the extent that it killed my pancreas and finally drained all my energy.

It was not until I understood Abraham's message that I realised I just had to let go of the cork. I meditated for a long time to help me recognise my cork. But even when I started to understand, I kept on punishing myself for being weak and not good enough, thereby pulling my cork underwater as soon as it reached the surface. Finally, I realised that I need to be selfish so that I remember to make my feelings my highest priority. If I forget to put on my own oxygen mask before helping others, I won't last very long.

Your Turn

Most people encounter stressful periods at times in their lives. Many young women these days suffer from stress, as they have become very determined to be successful at school and work and also want to look slim and beautiful. Not being able to relax, they block their energy and their cells' communication with the Source, causing pain in both their bodies and minds.

Look at your own situation to see how you can relax yourself and make your feelings your highest priority by using the tools you now have.

> **MANTRA:** When I am stressed or feel negativity, I can ask myself, "Is there a better way to view my situation?"

—That's it for now.

NEXT TIME:

- How to overcome addiction
- Why is it important to forgive?
- The power of our thoughts

NINTH JOURNEY
TOGETHER

ADDICTION

We can become addicted not just to drugs or alcohol, but also to other pursuits such as shopping, sex, gambling, exercise, work and food.

It's not an addiction until we have lost control, letting the things we do control us. Being able to take back control has, once again, everything to do with the way we think and feel.

Addiction is a signal that we have lost connection with our inner being as an extension of the Source. To soothe the pain that we feel after blocking the communication between our cells and the Source, we get hooked on something that we find soothing. The pain we are feeling is a sign that our view of ourselves and our world is out of sync with the way our inner being views us. As soon as we are able to close the gap between our inner being and ourselves by letting go of the cork, we will, however, find relief.

Being able to love yourself in the same way your inner being loves you will require you to be willing to listen to your feelings and to use those feelings as your guide. By prioritising how you feel and using the techniques that you have been practising to heighten your vibrations, even the strongest addiction can be cured. By being determined to monitor your thoughts, making sure that you start soothing them as soon as your feelings drop, you make sure that you are on the right track.

Everything has to do with where on the scale of emotions we choose to find ourselves. Using drugs, sex, eating disorders or gambling to get relief from our pain or to find pleasure in life might work for a while, but when we can't control it anymore, the fun is over.

To be able to choose differently, you need to believe that you'll feel better by stopping your habit. If you don't believe your life will change for the better, or if you don't see the problem with having the habit, it's not worth trying to stop an addiction.

The first step is to lift your emotions and see your life as objectively as possible. Then you can see if change is needed. You'll need to believe your habit is hindering you in your life progress, and you'll need to see the benefits of stopping your addiction to achieve a better life.

The next step is finding someone who has been through the process before. It's good to have somebody to cheer you on and keep you motivated on your journey towards change.

If you don't know anybody inspiring, doing the following assignment on your own is another option. As you move yourself up the scale of emotions, you will soon attract the right people and situations to help you to reach your goal.

ASSIGNMENT 25

Look objectively at your life to see if there are some habits that you would be better off without.

You might need professional help quitting a serious addiction (a twelve-step program, NA, AA, rehab, etc.); however, nobody can help you until you want to change. Use this opportunity to make up your mind about whether you need outside help.

If this assignment is enough, make a daily routine implementing all the tools you have learned to keep your feelings at the higher vibrations. Also, use the "Forum for Change" and "Feel Good" videos on my website: **www.a-life-worth-living.org**.

On the days you manage to love yourself and the world around you, you will feel good. If you manage to stay away from your "quick fix" for thirty consecutive days, you are a long way towards the goal of freedom and a good, conscious and meaningful life.

My Turn

Many people today suffer from various types of thought disorders, such as ADHD, OCD, tics, mania, depression, and anxiety. All are diagnoses that modern medicine finds almost impossible to cure. It can only reduce the impact through medication.

One of the reasons people use tranquilisers, sex, food, alcohol and gambling as medicine is that they don't know how to work with themselves and their own mindsets. Another reason is that many people simply do not believe in their inner beings and their own power, and therefore are not willing to learn how to change their mindsets. It is then easy to use simpler solutions in the form of pills or other external stimuli that they believe will help them to dull the inner turmoil or the pain they feel.

When I was sick and struggled with depression and anxiety, I received prescriptions for antidepressants and Valium tablets from my doctor. I benefited greatly from my medication at the beginning. However, I gradually lost faith in them, as I felt they had become an emotional crutch. The only thing they did for me was cushion the underlying problems and make me dozy without making me well. As mentioned, it was not until I became aware of my own mindset and decided to change my thoughts that my life became really good.

Valium and sleeping tablets are addictive agents that many people use as aids to calm down and relax their negative thought patterns. These types of medications can be lifesavers, but, if they are not combined with self-mastery techniques, the use of tranquilisers can gradually get out of control and make life worse.

With this as a backdrop, I've seen how important it is to monitor my own thoughts, not least as a preventive effect, but also to lift myself as quickly as possible when I sink into the low vibrations. Tranquilisers can nevertheless be useful in periods when life really dips into the dark side and we are too weak to lift ourselves, so I don't want to discourage anyone from using them. On the other hand, if you are a person who is struggling with addiction, be sure to factor this in when you are discussing prescriptions with your doctor.

Either way, before you decide to take medication, you should try to determine whether the medicine will be useful for you. Wait if you are uncertain. Our medicines will have a much better effect if we believe in them. If we are uncertain and concerned, we can get all kinds of side effects. Remember, you can make yourself sick and healthy just through thought.

At the moment, I am working on getting sufficient control of my mind to enable me to heal from diabetes. In addition, while I live in hope of a miracle, I try to move my mind away from the pain and choose to focus on good moments. I think about all the opportunities I have to live a good, conscious and meaningful life, in spite of the disease. The idea is that the more focus I have on pleasure and new opportunities, the more joy and new opportunities will become part of my life. Whether I'm dependent on insulin would then not be so much of an issue.

In other words, if you feel that your medicines really help you and you know that they have a good effect on your life, there is no purpose in ending what actually works, even if your dream is to be independent of medication. However, if you see that the drugs or things you do to master the disease are not working, it's time to look for new solutions.

Your Turn

You might not have a severe addiction, but anything that has started to rule your life and stop you from feeling happy is worth looking into. See if you can change it by monitoring your feelings and your level of vibrations.

If you suffer from a major addiction problem, it's important not to focus on your "quick fix." Nor should you dwell on things that don't work, as heavy depressive thoughts just suck the energy out of you. Instead, it will help to fully focus on the life you desire and every step you can take towards your dream. Each smile you share with others and every smile that is returned, every good thought, every good moment and every good day will be a victory and proof that you are heading for the life you dream about. This good feeling will fill you with energy and soothe you up to the high vibrations, where more good experiences await you.

And when you *don't* feel so good, you can use your mantras for self-sooth-ing: "This will also pass," "Nothing is so bad that it's not good for anything," "It could be a lot worse," etc. By focusing on the direction you want to go, instead of where you have been, you will not so easily make mistakes and you will keep an even steadier course towards your goal.

> **MANTRA:** I rely on aids outside myself only because I shut the door to my inner being.

(No one has such a strong focus that they always keep the door open to their inner being and their feelings. However, most of us are able to train ourselves to keep the door open much more often than we currently do.)

If You Would Like to Create a Support Group:

You might want to use this guide to create a support team around your challenges. Having like-minded people to share ideas and goals with can be motivating and inspiring. If you do this, the focus must be on the solution rather than the problem, so your conscious change can make you proud of who you are and what you *actually* accomplish in life. The meeting could start with the members of the group saying a variation of:

"My name is (Nina). I go in and out of balance just like everyone else, but, in this life, I have possibly chosen a bigger challenge than most.

My desire is to learn from my challenges and use them consciously as a spring-board to reach the goals of my life. At this point, my goals are to love myself, to love the people and the world that surrounds me and to let the challenges that I have chosen myself lift me to new heights. I plan to do this by taking respon-sibility for my feelings, one conscious thought at a time.

When I'm feeling low, I know that I can choose to use my tool kit, which in turn will help me move toward the top of the scale of emotions and my goal. I come to this group for help and eventually to help others gain more awareness and good and meaningful lives."

During the meeting, spend five minutes on Qigong and fifteen minutes on a guided meditation. The meeting can then be rounded off with everyone saying what they are grateful for and maybe a little about their own progress. If there is enough time, let someone tell their story.

If you are really struggling and feel down, include a mentor in the group to give you personal help in the use of the techniques this guide offers. (See how to become a mentor on my website, or consider finding a mentor on the forum). It's important to be honest when you struggle, but, more importantly, to shift your focus to enable you to take your life in a positive direction as quickly as possible.

A ritual from South-Sudan could be worth trying: the bad story was written down in detail and then burned to ashes. I'll talk about this more in the next chapter.

The Guide to A Life Worth Living can be applied to all challenges we want to address, whether the challenge is anxiety, addiction, depression or another illness.

The point must be, however, that we move the focus from the problem to the solution and use loving thoughts as a tool instead of focusing on fear, criticism and shame.

FORGIVENESS

Forgiveness does not mean accepting the wrongdoings of others or ourselves, but rather finding the peace within to allow us to continue our life journey. Depression, resentment, hate and rage are often the way to reach forgiveness, but forgiveness needs to be the goal, as without it our lives will feel stagnant and we'll never stop feeling pain.

Being able to close the gap between the way you see a person who has made a mistake and the way the Source sees this person is the only way to happiness. The Source loves us all, even if we don't love ourselves. We are all an extension of the Source, although few of us remember our origin and many of us get lost on our way.

Making mistakes is the way you learn. From the experience of what you don't like, you learn what you do like. Any time you are wronged it is therefore a gift that can, if you let it, help you to understand what you want from life. However, most of us struggle to see wrongdoing as a gift.

When you know what you do like, you put the Source into a creative mood. However, because of the Law of Attraction, you will not be able to receive what you like from life until you are able to vibrate on the level where this new creation exists. If you feel hateful towards a person who did you wrong, you are not able to vibrate high and therefore you won't be able to receive what you want. If you choose to forgive, on the other hand, you are again on your way up the scale of emotions in the direction of your dream.

Some people will not be able to experience the creation of their desires in *this* life, as they are not yet able to put themselves in a receptive mood by heightening their vibrations. They will, however, get as many chances as they like if they decide to take on a new body to go for another ride. That way, none of our pain needs to be wasted. If you decide not to forgive and that you would rather stay with the pain, it's your own choice. Another option is to put yourself in a receptive mood by forgiving and living your dream life now.

Some time back, I was invited on one of Narcotics Anonymous' summer excursions. Here, I came into contact with a woman who felt that God despised her because of all her sins.

I told the woman that I consciously choose to believe that I can't sin but only make mistakes. I also told her that I had chosen to believe that we and the whole universe are part of what we call "God" or "the Source."

The woman looked at me, confused but interested. So, I continued and explained that I use a picture to simplify my own understanding of God by comparing the universe with a human body where God is the brain and the "common mortal" people are the cells in the left hand of the body of the universe.

"The cells in the left hand of the body of the universe?" The woman was sceptical. She puzzled a little over what I had just said before she asked again, "Who's in the right hand, then?"

"The prophets," I replied.

"What prophets?" the woman asked.

"Jesus, Muhammad, Buddha, maybe Gandhi, all the people who know they are part of the universe's body and who have direct contact with God, who is the brain of the universe."

"What about the left hand cells? Why don't they know they are part of God?" the woman asked.

"Because most left hand cells are not willing to listen to their inner beings. Instead, they believe that they are alone and that they sin and are inferior because they are constantly reminded of all their mistakes and therefore are not able to accomplish the same as the right hand cells can."

"But without the left hand cells, the body of the universe would be handicapped," the woman exclaimed.

"Precisely. The universe would not manage to develop in the same way without the left hand and our help. But as soon as we begin to discover who we are and what we are a part of, we'll be able to train ourselves to become as skilled as the right hand. We'll then improve our ability to learn from mistakes and, in this way, we'll move steadfastly towards a good and loving world."

The woman stared at me with tears in her eyes and a big smile around her mouth.

"The thing is," I continued, and wiped away a tear from my own eye, "the universe will depend on a constant flow of new mistakes. Without imbalance and contrast, our development will stop."

"So, you think God will forgive me for all that crap I've inflicted on others?" the woman asked hopefully.

I shook my head. The woman stared, frustrated, at me before looking down at her hands sadly. The energy that had slowly but surely begun to build up inside her was now moving back to the basement again, so I hurried to add, "God, or what I've chosen to call the Source, has never considered you, or any other person for that matter, to be a sinner.

Therefore, there is no need to ask God for forgiveness. However, you'll need your own forgiveness. Until you are able to forgive yourself and understand who you really are, you will not be able to let go of the pain and allow yourself to have a good life."

ASSIGNMENT 26

Decide whether you want to forgive yourself or others for what you or they have done.

My Turn

Working in South-Sudan during the war, I experienced so much horror that it's hard to believe that forgiveness can even be an option.

Some of my sweet, young girls from the centre where I worked were gang-raped to the extent that they needed surgery. Feeling totally humiliated and crushed, they were not able to smile or laugh, always sitting with their legs crossed to protect themselves from more harm. Seeing the transformation in these girls after the centre leader had worked with them was like watching a miracle in the making.

As soon as the girls were ready to talk, which could take a long time, the centre leader took notes as the girls described what had happened. When everything was down on paper, they conducted a ceremony in which the girls burned the paper. The centre leader asked the girls to watch closely as the paper crumbled to ashes, telling them that burning their stories would remove the pain from their bodies and that it would never again be able to harm them. After the ceremony, the stories would be treated as if they had never happened, and the girls' emotions returned to normal.

I don't know if this way of removing pain would work in the western world, as the normal reaction would be to get the bad guy who made the mistake and to feel sorry for the victims. Feeling like a victim will, however, ensure that we'll never be able to let go of our pain, and if we can't get the guy and lock him up, we'll surely feel insecure for the rest of our lives.

On the other hand, believing that we are able to escape situations that vibrate in the lowest part of the scale of emotions by monitoring our feelings and keeping them high, we should be able to take back our power and no longer consider ourselves victims. This will increase our quality of life and our opportunity to live good and meaningful lives.

Your Turn

You might not have attracted situations this far down on the scale of emotions, but you might have experienced painful situations that you've still not been able to release. This is your chance to let go of the burden. In other words: will you allow yourself to see the situation with new eyes and give yourself permission to be happy, or will you choose to keep the pain? The choice of forgiveness is yours, as nobody else can make this choice for you.

Many people don't take responsibility for everything that happens to them. This is because they think that nobody would choose to be raped, mistreated or born into war and poverty. Such a thought is correct to a certain extent. People do not consciously choose specific acts of suffering; they just do not know the importance of lifting themselves up when they notice that they vibrate low.

Some when standing in the non-physical and considering which body, country, parents and social status they are going to go for, actually choose incredibly tough challenges consciously. They do this to help the Earth in its evolution towards a better, freer and more loving world, Abraham explains.

We also see people who consciously choose tough challenges as they live on Earth, like those who consciously choose to go into a war or those who choose to blow themselves to pieces because of their own convictions. Such choices are, however, taken from low vibrations, where people do not understand who they are or that we are all one.

Other challenges come from high vibrations. Mandela chose reconciliation rather than revenge. Rosa Parks didn't accept no for an answer and refused to move away from the bus seat reserved for whites. Both acted on the basis of high vibrations and the realisation that we are all equal and that we all come from the same source.

MANTRA: Through forgiveness, I give myself peace of mind so that I can concentrate on my own life journey towards change.

THE POWER OF YOUR THOUGHTS

When we understand how powerful our thoughts are, we should guard them in the best possible way, leaving out fearful news or programs and keeping ourselves with like-minded people.

If you can't escape bad news and negative people, it helps to be extra careful, knowing there will always be people who are too frightened to believe in the power of their own thoughts and therefore become easy prey for fear.

The trick is to stay focused and not allow yourself to be dragged down the drain with them. Staying focused for a long time in a negative environment is challenging but still possible; you just need to monitor your feelings more closely.

Getting out into nature and keeping a pet can lift your spirits. Both are highly recommended. Just the smell of a flower or the wag of a dog's tail can lift your vibrations. Listening to uplifting music and being conscious of not indulging in all the depressing lyrics out there will also help to keep your thoughts up in the high vibrations. When you feed your mind with fearful or melancholic thoughts, you just make it harder to feel good.

So, being conscious is the way to happiness and the creation of all good things and situations. However, as none of us are perfect, we will not be able to be conscious at all times. We will slip and fall, over and over again, as it's easy to engage in fearful discussions or listen to sad songs and go down the drain along with negative people. You might even be the one who drags others down. In any case, tomorrow is a brand-new day to try to stay conscious.

Tomorrow, you'll again try to stay positive and focused and maybe you'll get a bit further into your day before you fail. What will keep you motivated is the knowledge that, for every day you try to keep yourself conscious, you get closer to finally living your dream. Being angry or disappointed in yourself for falling will only make the situation worse, as the chain of falling, getting up again, and falling again is the only way to move ourselves and this world forward.

You might wonder why the Source could not make us conscious and flawless from the beginning, so we don't have to go through so much pain. But then, you have forgotten that everything, including the Source, constantly evolves and will always change towards a better version of itself.

It is us people who have the active role in this process, while the souls of the non-physical existence have the role of supervisors, Abraham explains. The fact is that we humans are not so keen to follow the guidance we receive from the non-physical, as humanity has not yet understood who we really are.

To create the best possible basis for growth in the everlasting expansion of the universe, human beings have been given full freedom to choose where we want to focus. We have also been given full freedom to determine our own developmental speed.

If we take a closer look at developments on Earth, we will discover that there has actually been a formidable improvement only in recent generations. There have never been so few wars in the world, so little poverty and so many getting the opportunity for education and, as a consequence, freedom to live the lives they want.

COVID has been a huge challenge for the entire population on Earth. In time, hopefully we will see something good coming out of it.

The problem is that humanity largely focuses on what does not work, and forgets to appreciate all the improvement that is happening around us. In this way, we unfortunately miss out on many opportunities to feel joy and gratitude. Life can then feel unnecessarily heavy and difficult.

If we manage to see life from an eternity perspective, on the other hand, it does not matter much if development does not go faster than it already does. Abraham says that evolution on Earth goes at exactly the speed it should. We are not here to fix something that does not work; we are here to further develop the Earth towards an ever better, freer and more loving world. And since we have all eternity as a timeframe, there is really nothing urgent.

ASSIGNMENT 27

Think of an example of a time where you went down the drain. Find out how to do it differently to prevent yourself from falling into the same trap over and over again.

My Turn

I'm quite new in this quest for good thoughts and feelings. However, every day I'm learning more about how not to fall into the trap of low-vibrating creations. Not too long ago I had a spiral of bad thoughts and one bad thought gave birth to one bad situation after another.

Looking closer at my own bad creations taught me a lesson. One August, just ten days after I moved to Addis, I was very happy to get involved in the Ethiopian International Film Festival. During the third month, I discovered that my involvement in the festival might distract me from my writing, and a tiny spark of fear was created. Getting closer to the end of the festival, with the big reward ceremony coming up, it became so hectic that none of the people involved had time to rest, and writing during my spare time became, of course, impossible.

Living out of my suitcase for several months had also taken its toll on my nerves, as our container was stuck in customs.

During the final weekend of the festival, I caught a terrible cold, but, at that point, there was no way I could stay at home. Thinking that as soon as the festival was over I would be able to nurse my aching body, I managed to pull myself through the Ethiopian "Oscars" ceremony. The morning after the festival was over, I got a message saying we had to leave the place where we had been living temporarily in Ethiopia, as our more permanent home in Addis was now ready for us to move into.

The plan was to leave for South Africa in three days to celebrate Christmas there. I used my last days in Addis to unpack every single item from the container. With the cold now hammering my head and body worse than ever, I felt terribly sorry for myself.

The first thing that happened after I parked the rental car outside my home in South Africa was that I twisted my ankle. I was extremely tired at that point, with my head spinning with worries about all the things I had to do before my family arrived, making me unaware of where I was putting my feet. However, it was not until I got a terrible rash all over my whole body and face that I stopped and asked myself, "What am I doing?" Suddenly, I was able to see that I had gotten myself into a spiral of bad creations.

I had not yet understood how incredibly important it was to switch focus when things are not going well. Instead of concentrating on all the great aspects of my life, such as being part of an "Oscars" ceremony, getting a beautiful home to live in, having so many great things to unpack, and having a fantastic family to celebrate Christmas with, my focus had mainly been on all my worries, and I had cleverly managed to attract even more of them.

Becoming aware of my spiral of bad creations, I stopped and spent some time in meditation. I also made a long list of all the things I was grateful for, and after that I managed to turn the bad spiral into a fortunate one, mainly creating opportunities for good timing, good situations and great people to come into my life. Every now and then, I slip and fall, but when I do, I try to quickly start guarding my thoughts and feelings, looking for positive aspects in my life.

Your Turn

Go into detail about a time in your life when things did not go so well. See if you can discover why you experienced the snowball effect of bad creations and how you could have done things differently by keeping your vibrations up.

> **MANTRA:** My focus is reflected in what happens to me.

—That's it for now

NEXT TIME

- How to relax during the process of dying
- How to find pleasures in the small things in life
- How a random act of kindness can change your life

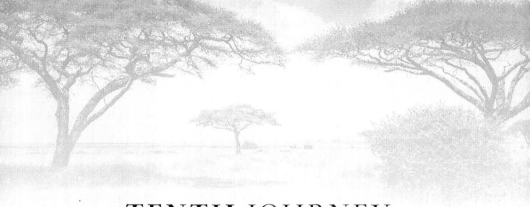

TENTH JOURNEY
TOGETHER

LIFE CYCLE

At some stage, we all need to die to make room for a new life. However, becoming terminally ill before we feel we are ready to leave our bodies can be a devastating experience. On the other hand, if we choose to believe in eternity and in our souls or inner beings as extensions of the Source, we might be able to find peace while preparing for our last day.

If we are able to believe that we will never leave our loved ones, but rather strengthen our relationships with the ones we struggle to leave behind, most of us will feel relief.

Abraham Hicks explains that every time we go to sleep, we meet up with our friends and relatives in the non-physical, getting refilled with their love and appreciation for our expansion.

No matter what your choices are, the non-physical will not judge you. Instead, they will guide you using your feelings as a tool. An unpleasant feeling will, sooner or later, lead to an understanding of what you really want from this life experience and will move you to a new level of physical expansion.

How much you are able to remember from your nights with the non-physical depends on how conscious you are while you're awake. By getting in touch with your feelings, you are able to utilise the guidance you are given from the non-physical.

The thought of being able to support your loved ones from the non-physical will make it easier for you to leave them behind as you prepare for your new journey. You can then use your energy to prepare yourself, instead of using these last moments on sorrow, fear, bitterness and frustration.

It might also feel good to believe that, in the non-physical, we still have a purpose, as all our focus is still here on Earth where the universe expansion is created. With this belief, we also understand in greater depth the importance of our life here on Earth.

When you enter a new body, you are like an astronaut taking the first step on the moon. But, instead of having the whole world focus on your discoveries on the moon, you have your soul-group in the non-physical supporting you as you make your discoveries on Earth. In this way, your life will never end. You just withdraw from your physical, painful body to take on a new role and give somebody else the chance to make their discoveries on Earth. Finally, when you are ready for a new adventure, it's just a case of picking a body and going for a new ride.

By choosing to believe that we can decide when to die, many people have miraculously recovered from the most incurable of health issues. However, if we find we are done here on Earth and decide we need a break, or if our inner beings know that we'll be more useful somewhere else, we will exit this Earthly experience.

Making the choice to leave our bodies is usually not a conscious decision, as most people are afraid of dying or find it difficult to leave their loved ones behind. Believing in an eternal life and that you are leaving for new adventures elsewhere might make leaving your body easier, as you now know that you play an important role both with and without it.

ASSIGNMENT 28

Look back over your life and try to find examples of the non-physical interacting with you.

My Turn

My mother sat at the window of our cottage by the fjord watching our old neighbour rowing his small, open boat towards his favourite fishing spot. Noticing that there was a young man with the neighbour, my mum felt relieved, as she had always been worried that the old man would fall into the sea.

At the fishing spot, our neighbour prepared his fishing net and rose to his feet to throw the net out into the water. The young man got to his feet too, as if to protect the old man from falling. My mum stared, stressed about the two men, thinking that neither of them should have been standing in such a small boat; however, the young man looked like he would be able to save them both if they fell into the ice-cold water.

After a while, my mother started to wonder who the young man could be, as she had never seen him before. She turned in her chair and called my dad over to see if he knew the young man. My father came into the living room and gazed at the boat, but he could only see our old neighbour. When my mother turned back and looked towards the small rowing boat, she was not able to see the young man either. Thinking that he must have fallen into the sea, my mother rose quickly to her feet but, after seeing the old man sit down, take the oars and slowly lift his head and smile at her, she knew that the young man was only our old neighbour's guardian.

* * *

During the time we were living in Uganda, a very good friend of our family was terminally ill with cancer. My husband, the children and I went to say goodbye, as we thought our friend would not be alive the next time we visited Norway.

As we tried to say our final goodbyes before leaving, my youngest son asked our friend if he could give him a sign when leaving his body. We all smiled, a bit surprised by the question, but our friend promised he would let us know when he left.

Sitting on the terrace in Kampala eating breakfast a few months later, my husband looked up at the sky. "What's happening?" he asked, surprised. Our youngest son ran eagerly into the garden, staring up at the sky. Thousands of white herons covered the sky, blocking out the sun as they passed over the roof of our house. A few minutes later, the phone rang; our friend had just died.

Your Turn

You might not be terminally ill, but most of us know somebody who has died and, as all of us are going to die sooner or later, it can be helpful to look into your own experiences to see if you can find evidence of non-physical existence in your life. Being able to believe in the non-physical makes it easier to both live and to let go of a sick body.

> **MANTRA:** I am never alone and I will always live, with or without a physical body.

THE SMALL PLEASURES IN LIFE

When we are able to enjoy the small things in life, our happiness will be unlimited, as the whole world is packed with things to be happy about.

Previously, you made a list of things you are grateful for, and this is somewhat along the same lines; however, looking closely at all the small details, you'll be able to fill every second of your life with pleasure.

Earlier today, I sat outside in the hammock, patting my dog. I played a game with him as I fed him some biscuits. If people had not known me, they would have thought me totally nuts, as I was laughing and screaming with joy every time my dog managed to catch his treats. Lying down in the hammock, I watched a sunbird swing on a thin branch up in the top of the acacia tree in my garden. Seeing how the bird enjoyed life, I was suddenly back to my own childhood, when I used to sit on the swing, enjoying the ride and not having a worry in the world.

As a small child, I could let myself be fascinated by a stone, a leaf or a small insect, spending time watching it, feeling the texture, smelling it and sometimes tasting it. Today, some people call this mindfulness or, as Eckhart Tolle calls it, "Being in the NOW." When we focus in this way, leaving all our worries behind, our cells have free access to the Source and our bodies and minds thrive.

ASSIGNMENT 29

Look for something that you find interesting to focus on and leave all other thoughts behind. In your journal/workbook, register how this kind of focus makes your body and mind feel.

My Turn

As a youngster, I played this game all the time. I particularly remember how I could sit in my Grandmother Nelly's bed absorbing all the details of her room, from sight, to smell, to sound and also to how things felt under my small, soft fingers.

Every summer, I slept in my grandmother's bed when we visited my father's family on their tiny, old farm. The farm was built in the early eighteenth century and was characteristic of those faraway days, both in the way that it was constructed and the way that it smelled.

I remember this small cosy house and the short, creaking bed, down to the two linen pillowcases embroidered with an *N* for Nina and an *N* for Nelly. It smelled sweet from the sun and hot iron and felt soft between my small fingers from wear and tear.

I remember Aunt Alma's bed on the other side of the bedroom. It was a worn out, mustard-coloured, antique, velvet sofa with very poor suspension, making Aunt Alma lie in an almost sitting position, which the doctor had said was good for her weak heart. Every morning, Grandmother would wash old Aunt Alma from a sink bowl in front of the antique mirror and plait her hip-long grey-and-black hair before dressing her like an old doll made of porcelain.

Sitting in the bed, watching the relaxed atmosphere of the room, I felt the rhythm of my heart was in total harmony with the rhythm and harmony of the room and everything in it, from the warm sunbeams that lit up the room through the open window to the sound of a big, fat fly flapping its wings on the windowsill, to the birds' morning song and the pictures of Jesus, Grandpa and Napoleon hanging in dark, brown frames over Grandma's bed. They all echoed happily inside my small body.

When Grandma and Aunt Alma had left the room, I would slide quietly out of the high bed, bend down and carefully drag the porcelain chamber pot out from under the sofa. If it was warm and too full and I was afraid I might slosh urine out on the floor, I would leave the pot and jump out of the low-set window, avoiding the nettles, and run barefoot in the cool grass, wet from morning dew, to the outhouse on the other side of the yard.

Coming out of the outhouse after finishing my business, I would enthusiastically open the door and leap out from the dark, cool room. I would enjoy the morning sun, feeling how it warmed my body while I swirled around and around with my eyes squinting against the blue sky's sparkling white sun rays.

From here, I would eagerly look for red, ripe strawberries. I would pick a berry with my chubby little hand, bring it to my tiny nose and smell, while thinking, "Nothing in the world smells as good as strawberries!" Then, I would feel the moisture of the berry against my fingers, study the characteristic shape and, finally, I would taste the sweet ripeness of the fruit on my tongue before letting it slide slowly down to my stomach.

From this passionate moment, my day began, and it also ended with joy and passion for the beautiful world I was a part of. By taking time to enjoy everything in my small world, I've never been happier.

Your Turn

Find something in your surroundings to give your full attention to and see how it makes you feel. Taking your time to really enjoy the details of this world's creations will soon make your soul soar.

> **MANTRA:** When I release my own negative thoughts and instead let myself be fascinated by the beautiful details of this world, I open myself to the love and guidance of my inner being and the Source.

ACT OF KINDNESS

Even something as simple as a smile can make our world shine. A smile delivered or received from the heart makes us happy. A smile or a nice comment takes no effort at all but it feels so good to give and to receive.

Why it feels so good, I believe, is because the Source sees us as one. It is the Source that connects us. Kindness towards anything in creation opens the communication between our cells. We literally feel the oneness with the Source when our cells start vibrating, and the feeling of high vibrations echoing back and forth makes us feel happy and connected.

Being grateful and patient is another way of showing kindness. Helping someone takes more effort and is often misunderstood. However, if the one who gives the help does it from the heart, and the one who receives wants the help, it works marvellously. The problem is when one of the parties does not want to give or receive.

To become conscious of why you give and also how you receive is important because if you don't do it from the heart, you drain yourself of energy, or, in other words, you stop the communication between your cells and the Source. This is why it's always good to become conscious of why you do something before acting.

A smile comes spontaneously, whereas helping someone takes energy if you don't do the act from love. By doing any act out of obligation, you drain yourself of love and energy. If you do your act from love, you fill yourself with love and energy and you feel at one with the Source.

Using a random act of kindness as an easy way of filling yourself with love and energy is smart, although it requires you to be conscious of why you are doing it.

You no longer need to rely on others to be kind towards you because you can choose to be kind to others. By doing so, you can lift yourself up. In addition, you may also raise others' emotions, if the person you are trying to uplift is able to receive.

If you are really, really conscious, you don't even need the gratitude of others. You can decide yourself if their gratitude is necessary to ensure that you still feel good. This knowledge gives you total freedom from the outside world and lets you understand that it's up to you alone if you want to feel happy.

ASSIGNMENT 30

Look at how you can fill yourself with energy and love with a random act of kindness. Find something that makes you happy and use it whenever you feel the need for love and energy.

My Turn

I have seen it happen that a man has held open a door for a woman and she has reacted in a negative way, as if his holding the door meant she wasn't able to open the door on her own. In a situation like this, it's helpful to know that our act of kindness is not only to be kind and loving towards somebody else, but also to be kind and loving towards ourselves.

We are all responsible for our own happiness and it's someone's own loss if they don't use an act of kindness towards them as a chance to be grateful. However, to judge a reaction like this is difficult, as we don't know why the woman reacted as she did. She might have had a rough day, and maybe she'd had a humiliating experience based on gender sometime earlier in her life. Keeping ourselves from judging and being patient and understanding will just give us a new chance to fill ourselves with love, happiness and energy.

· · ·

When I'm out and about, I like to smile at people, as seeing their facial expressions change from sad or serious to happy in a fraction of a second makes my soul soar. Still, it happens occasionally that some people don't return my smile. Then I try to think that they may not have understood that I smiled at them or they may simply not have enough energy to be able to receive.

I also like to give people good feedback for jobs well done, as I know it makes us all feel more confident when we receive positive responses. To give my soul a chance to soar, I try to be conscious of giving myself the opportunity to be kind as often as possible.

On the other hand, I don't go out of my way to help others if I feel the act of kindness will drain me of my own energy. If I'm not up to speed with the vibrations of an act of kindness, I find it very difficult to do it. This is a balance, since sometimes I know that such an action could actually help give me energy. The problem is that I'm too tired at that point to see how giving and receiving really fit together.

Helping others and believing they need my help is, however, an inferior act and is unhelpful in the long run. To believe in others and help them to believe in themselves is a much better choice.

Your Turn

I believe we all often do random acts of kindness no matter what. However, it's helpful to think of them as a tool to make not only others feel happy, but also to make yourself happy. This way, you will no longer need to wait for others to make you feel good.

> **MANTRA:** Good deeds are gifts first and foremost to myself.

—That's it for now.

NEXT TIME:

- Counting your miracles
- Looking into the mirror and smiling
- Giving yourself the opportunity to soar

ELEVENTH JOURNEY
TOGETHER

"MIRACLES"

I believe it's time to start counting our miracles and get used to recognising them, as, I believe, the quicker we notice that they are part of our lives, the more miracles we will experience.

If you have never experienced a "miracle," it can be really hard to believe that they happen. If you think that what you can't explain is just a coincidence, it's understandable that you don't realise the significance that such an episode may have in your life.

If I had not experienced my own miracles or things I couldn't explain, I would not believe half of what I read. However, after having so many strange experiences myself, I have no problem believing that Joe Dispenza in the United States, for example, is running around as healthy as a fish after smashing his spine and being destined to never walk again. While it is a bit more difficult to believe the story of how Dispenza restored his spine, I'm now able to consider even this to be truthful.

What this man did was believe in his own thoughts and his ability to communicate with his cells and, in doing so, he built up his own spine, vertebrae by vertebrae, just by using his thoughts and visualisation.

Joe Dispenza's book *You Are the Placebo* is really worth reading, regardless of whether you face major physical challenges or not. This book is a wonderful testimony to the power of thought.

I heard an interview with Anita Moorjani, who walked out of the hospital a few weeks after going into a coma because her body was totally rotting with cancer. During her coma, she understood why she had become ill and decided to take back her health and tell her story.

The story she told in her interview is one of the sources of inspiration for this guide. Anita Moorjani said that it was her thoughts that had made her sick, but, with a new conviction and understanding of how life really worked, she became miraculously cured. Doctors could not even see traces of the cancer that, five weeks earlier, had been about to kill her.

Anita Moorjani later wrote the book *Dying to Be Me*. It is worth reading, regardless of whether you are sick or healthy. (You can also listen to Anita telling her story on this book's website under "Health.")

Faith is a conviction that we can choose consciously, yet we need to convince ourselves that what we believe is right or possible. Sometimes, we need more evidence to enable us to change our faith. We can do this by focusing on the evidence that builds around what we wish to believe in until we manage to convince ourselves that what we want is actually possible.

Some say that faith can move mountains. Even if we think that this statement is exaggerated, what we want to believe has great influence on us. That's why it is important to consciously choose the thoughts that can control our lives.

We can choose to believe we are weak, unsuccessful and ill and focus on anything that seems to prove it. Or we can choose to believe that we are strong, healthy and successful and find evidence for this instead.

I have had periods in my life where I chose to look for evidence that I was weak. However, after I started listening to Abraham's teaching, I chose to find evidence that I am strong. What is interesting is that I can be both strong and weak, depending on what evidence I am looking for. In other words, I'm exactly what I choose to believe I am.

I know that I have diabetes, but I have chosen to believe that one beautiful day there will be a cure for this disease. While I'm waiting for my miracle, I choose to believe I can have an excellent life despite being dependent on my insulin injections. In this way, the disease does not need to have much negative impact on my life – in fact, rather the opposite. Thanks to my diabetes, I am now aware of what I want to do with the remaining time I have left in my physical form.

Another example of why we should be careful about what we choose to believe is the story of Aunt Alma, the sister of my grandmother. At the age of forty, Alma was told by her doctor that she had a very weak heart. After this news, she did nothing but sleep, eat and sit. Grandma cared for her like a porcelain doll until Alma died over forty years later.

Nobody, except the doctor, noticed any signs that Aunt Alma's heart was weak. I don't know if Aunt Alma had a desire to get strong and healthy and if she believed in miracles. But what Alma really believed in was elves. Her belief was so strong she even claimed she could see them.

ASSIGNMENT 31

Look into your life and see if you can discover odd things that have happened to you – things you can't explain. Make a list and add to it when new, strange things happen.

My Turn

When I look back, I can see many episodes that I can't explain. None of them have to do with sickness and healing. However, they have made me realise that I'm not alone and that things that are happening may not be as random as they might appear. Whether you want to call them miracles or just inexplicable or strange episodes is up to you.

1. When I was around eight or nine years old, I had the first odd experience that I remember. I was walking my dog by the lake on a chilly spring day when an old, poor man with long hair and a beard passed me wearing sandals and a greyish robe like those from the time that Jesus lived. I thought it was a very strange outfit for a cold day.

For weeks and weeks, I thought of this man, regretting that I had not taken him home, fed him and given him some proper clothes and a haircut. This was in the sixties, and no one had long hair in my town. The man had looked so out of place and had looked at me as if he wanted me to take action and do something. But, of course, I didn't; I was only a young girl and he was an old man, and I didn't know how he or my family would have reacted if I had come home with this prehistoric man and asked my dad to cut his hair and my mum to change his clothes and feed him.

I have since wondered if this experience triggered my interest in helping others, especially the most vulnerable people of this world.

2. Just before I moved to Uganda, I was on the verge of making the biggest mistake of my life. Had I not changed course, I would have had no possibility of living and working the way I do today.

The only reason I stopped and changed my life to take it in a new direction was that a loud voice asked, "Nina, what are you doing?" The voice didn't come from outside but from inside my head, although it sounded like it came from outer space. The deafening voice didn't scare me though. I knew immediately that this voice wished me only good.

Today, I believe it was my inner being warning me away from ruining my opportunity to do the work I love.

3. In Uganda, I worked with street children and, through my good friends in Norway, we collected money to furnish a house to get the most vulnerable girls off the street. My friends collected so much money that we could also send the girls to school.

Just before the girls' exam, we ran out of money and none of the girls could take their exams until they had paid their exam fees. I felt devastated and didn't know what to do when one of the girls came up to me. She touched my arm softly, smiled and said, "With God, everything is possible." Looking at all the suffering in the world at that time, I didn't trust God. So I sadly smiled back to the girl, thinking, "Poor thing, there's no God that will allow you to take your exam."

On my way home from work, I felt an urge to pop into the bookshop. Ever since I was young, I have loved bookstores and I could sit on the floor of a shop reading books for hours. That day, I did not have much time for reading, but I felt like looking to see if there were any new and inspiring book titles on the shelves. On the first shelf I browsed, I saw a white book entitled *With God, Everything Is Possible*. In total disbelief, I took the book off the shelf and went to the cashier to pay for it. Walking home, I eagerly turned the pages to see what this book was all about.

Arriving home, I left the book on my desk and switched on my computer to check my emails. The first email I opened was from a friend in Norway, announcing that there was lots of money on the way to my account for the street children.

From that moment, I really started to believe that with God, everything is possible.

4. By getting so much money from my friend, I was now also able to start up a basic education program to give the teenagers who had never been to school an opportunity to learn how to read and write.

Fifty youths between thirteen and eighteen years old came walking from all over Kampala to join the school. Some of these kids had been living in a dry sewage pipe for a decade before they were helped out of their misery. They did not know how to count to three or write their names, but after seven months of coming to school three days a week, they were able to read and write. They spoke English and they could make budgets and run their own businesses.

Several of these teenagers are now running their own homes for street children in Kampala, and one has his own business in the United States.

5. As we had more money coming in from Norway, we also started a traditional dancing group, which some of the street children attended. Their

teacher was a former street child who, with his background, was able to totally transform these kids.

Because of AIDS, Kampala was flooded with street children at the beginning of this millennium and the government handled the situation extremely badly. The children were shot and killed, raped, run over deliberately by cars and imprisoned. Members of the dancing group became ambassadors for the problems street children were facing in Uganda. The group performed for ambassadors, ministers and the president, managing to change the way street children were treated in Uganda through dancing and setting up theatres telling their stories.

They also travelled all over the United States, and one of these children got an offer to become a professional dancer in Japan.

I believe this project was the first to use dance and drama to help disadvantaged children to gain faith in themselves.

6. Before we bought our property in South Africa, I wasn't sure if it was the right decision. Going back on the plane to Tanzania, where we lived at the time, I looked out of the window and into the air, asking myself why I had chosen to build a home in this country, of all places.

At the same moment that I asked the question, a rainbow turned itself into a circle, looking like a dartboard. Then, I saw the shadow of the plane going nose first into the bullseye. Just before traveling, I had won a Nordic competition playing darts. In Norway, we say that we have made our perfect shot if we hit the bullseye.

So, the answer to my question of why we should have bought this property in South Africa was that it was a perfect decision.

7. Last year, I had a strange experience standing at a red light in Cape Town looking into the eyes of a beggar. In a fraction of a second, I saw myself through the beggar's eyes, as if I was inside the beggar's body.

It made me know that we are all one.

8. Just a week ago, I told my husband's colleague my son's incredible story from when he travelled in Namibia. My son and his friends lost their car key in the sand dunes after slipping and sliding down a huge mountain of sand, and they did not discover their loss until they arrived back at the car.

Standing in the middle of the desert with no other cars around and with very little water left, my son was totally devastated. His two friends just concluded there was no way they could find the key in the sand, and that it would be even worse than looking for a needle in a haystack. Seeing the danger in the situation, my son decided not to listen to his friends and walked up the mountain of sand to look for the key anyway. He couldn't find it.

Before the sun left the sand dune, my son stared in desperation up the golden mountain and suddenly saw something glittering closer to the top. Filled with faith, he ran towards the peak of the huge sand dune and dug out the car key, which was totally covered by sand except for the tiny, shiny top part.

Just as I had finished my son's incredible story, my husband's colleague checked a message coming in on his phone. It said, "Never give up!" He showed me the message saying, "Strange. This message just came out of nowhere, like a comment on your story."

This last comment made me believe that all my out-of-the-normal experiences, or miracles, if you like, tell us not to give up, as there is always light at the end of a tunnel. It also tells me that we are never alone and that we just need to tune in to the messages that lead us in the right direction. And the right direction is always up, up towards the good and high vibrations where we find hope, happiness, enthusiasm, passion, joy, love, inner growth and freedom.

I could have written of many more small and large inexplicable episodes in my life, episodes that most people would dismiss as coincidences but that I have gradually started to interpret as guidance from my inner being. After spending some time looking back on my life, I believe that each of these events has influenced me to become the person I am today. So, who am I?

I have become a human being so keen to find out why I am here and how I can best use my life that I wrote a whole book on this subject.

It may seem like a coincidence that I was born on Easter morning, that the place I grew up was called the missionary ground because of the mission college in Stavanger, Norway. That my parents were concerned with the big questions in life and that one of my most interesting high school teachers told amazing stories from Madagascar, which inspired me once again to travel to Africa.

It may also be a coincidence that one of my very best friends was a Jehovah's Witness. Observing her life made me sceptical of organised religion's sin and Hell. From there, I went from not believing in any higher power to becoming increasingly interested in finding out if humankind is actually part of something bigger than itself.

When I look back on my life, I see that, regardless of whether this "thread" in my life is random or not, all the things I write about are, in any case, marked by my upbringing and my experiences. I think that if you look closely, you will also find a thread in your life that helps guide you in the direction that will make your life meaningful.

Your Turn

You might think that you haven't experienced any odd things or miracles. Many people don't feel support from the non-physical, as they don't pay attention to all the messages they are given. If you haven't been paying attention, you can start now; I believe you have infinite intelligence trying to get your attention, which would just love to support you if you ask.

> **MANTRA:** I am so free that I can choose to accept or refrain from the guidance given to me from the non-physical.

YOUR BODY

Looking at yourself in the mirror and being happy with your own reflection is not always easy. However, as we talked about earlier, being able to accept your body for what it is will make your life so much easier.

These days, we have a fixation with our bodies that makes our lives unnecessarily hard, and it's often one of the main obstacles that stops us from feeling happy. If we asked ourselves what we regard as beautiful, we would most likely have a totally different answer depending on who and what we are referring to. However, we usually find people beautiful regardless of their look when we love and respect them – and that's not to mention our dogs and cats! There are so many strange-looking pets out there that we just adore, which really proves that our look has nothing to do with how loveable we are.

Being able to love yourself regardless of your look is maybe the best gift you can give yourself. By loving yourself regardless of anyone else's opinions, you don't need anybody to endorse your worthiness. By being this confident, you'll definitely set yourself free. And **to set ourselves free is one of this journey's goals, as all our dreams include the dream of freedom.**

Ever since we were living in caves, we have been fighting for our freedom to grow and change in the direction of our own choice. However, freedom from our own judgement can only be handled by ourselves and, despite its manageability, it can be very difficult to not judge the vehicle we once chose to bring us the change and growth we're all seeking. Having said that, making ourselves happy when we look in the mirror with a new hairstyle, different clothes and good makeup can cheer us up. In addition, it brightens our surroundings and is an outlet for our creativity.

Looking back, it is quite natural to decorate our bodies with paint, clothing and ornaments. We have done this since the beginning of time. The difference now is that we tend to get too critical. When we dislike our bodies, we lose the joy of our bodily creations.

Having discovered the many colourful tribes living in the Omo Valley in southern Ethiopia, I fortunately see that there is still great freedom in beauty. The tribes of the Omo Valley use body paint and plants to decorate their bodies. Thy show us that we do not need a lot of money or a perfect body to create something that is beautiful. Regardless of what you might think of the Omo Valley body art, these bodily artworks reflect a wonderful diversity in this world. If you don't feel inspired by this art, I hope you will still feel happy to see how free some people are in relation to their bodies. (See links at the back of the book.)

Whatever you decide to do with your body, your creation will not make you happy unless you find your happy feelings before touching the canvas. This also applies if your dream is a beautiful body, as a great body can easily become a shell around a shallow and non-free interior.

Starting the day with something as easy as smiling to yourself in the mirror is an effective way to lift your vibrations. If you continue to be good to yourself throughout the day, you can finally reach the channel where your dreams and wishes can flow freely into your physical life. However, if you start your day by being critical towards yourself, the energy of your body will sink and you will close the door to the Vortex as soon as you see yourself in the mirror in the morning. In other words, enjoy your body and make the best of it.

ASSIGNMENT 32

Smile when you look at yourself in the mirror.

My Turn

Growing up, I loved to make people laugh with the funny faces that I can – and still do – make. However, sometimes I like to look beautiful. Sometimes I try too hard, and if I don't succeed, that can make me feel sad.

Recently, I discovered that the reason I don't find myself beautiful might be because I'm not happy as I look at myself in the mirror, and not the other way around.

When we are hopeful, joyous, peaceful, confident or knowledgeable, we reflect our inner beings and other people find us attractive regardless of our outer beauty. When our souls soar, there is no look that can stop us from being admired.

Your Turn

Try to remember to smile at your reflection and be kind to yourself. Starting your day by focusing on excess fat, bad hair or wrinkles is like bullying yourself. You wouldn't be so critical and mean to somebody you love, so why do it to yourself?

To feel energetic and to vibrate on a high frequency, you need all the love and happiness you can get. The thing is, you don't need others to tell you how great or beautiful you are. It's more than enough if you know from your heart that you are worthy just the way you are.

On the other hand, if you want to change your look, do it from a happy place. Know that, if you make any changes from unhappiness, the chances of your changes being a success are lower than if you make changes from a place of excitement and love towards yourself. In other words, heighten your vibrations first.

> **MANTRA:** I chose my body with all the challenges it may have. I also chose whether I want to make the best of it or neglect it and whether I will be dissatisfied with my own choice of body.

RELATIONSHIPS

We all encounter different types of relationships: our relationships with our parents, siblings, grandparents, friends, schoolmates, colleagues, neighbours, children and partners.

Some you choose yourself and some you don't remember having chosen. Whatever you feel about the people who surround you, you have, one way or another, attracted them into your life.

The best way to either keep these people close to you or let them slip into the distance is to heighten your vibrations. The people who are nice will stay, assuming that you have common wishes for where you want to go with your lives. If they don't stay, it could be because they deliberately want to take their lives in a new direction. Alternatively, it could be because they hold themselves in the lower vibrations and will automatically keep their distance from people in the higher vibrations, as they will find them very annoying.

However, if you live in the same house or work closely with someone operating in the lower vibrations, it's easy to be dragged down the drain with them. Being conscious of guarding your feelings can, in this case, be your only option. If you are lucky, they might choose to heighten their vibrations and come up to "play" with you.

If people you really dislike have only one positive thing about their personalities, choose to keep focus on this one thing. Every time you prepare to meet such a person, imagine in detail this one thing you like about the person you strive to have a good relationship with. As you learn to keep your focus on this particular positive personality trait, this will be your experience when you meet this person in the future.

Should this person not show any kind of positive personality traits, try to visualise them the way you want to see them. Personally, I have found such a strategy to work. However, it took me a lot of time before I succeeded. Sometimes it might not be worth the effort.

To better understand the dynamics between people, I find it helpful to believe that there is only one type of love, not different types depending on whether a person is our lover, child or neighbour. I also find it helpful to believe that all relationships that are going to feel good need to be built on love.

There are no limits to how many people we can love at the same time. Demanding that our partner not love anybody but us is against nature, as our inner being knows we are all one. Jealousy will just make our lives shallow and claustrophobic.

If we really want to spend time with someone, the best way is to attract them to us through our vibrations. If you are nice to spend time with, nobody can stop your lover, family or friends from wanting to be with you. If you instead guilt trip them and demand that they be only with you, the time spent together will not be fun.

I have also chosen to believe that having sex is not necessarily a sign of deep love. We can feel love towards many people without wanting to have sex with them. We can also have sex with people without making them our partners for the rest of our lives. Having said that, orgasm is one of the best ways we can become one with our inner beings. This, however, requires that we stay in the high vibrations during the sexual act.

If our relationship is not built on trust and freedom, we are not talking about love but about fear. As far as I can see, unfortunately many marriages are not loving relationships, but rather built on a fear-based contract that, after some years, drains energy and forces the couple to end the bondage. Feeling so much pain from our stagnant relationship, we often don't know of a better way of releasing the bad feelings than to run away from them.

If you are in a relationship where you plan to leave somebody, it's a good idea to use your tools to raise your vibrations before doing anything. Then check your feelings about remaining or leaving the one you once loved.

If you make any important decisions from the lower vibrations, you'll surely attract more pain. By lifting your vibrations first, you'll be able

to listen to your inner being, which will tell you to leave or stay by using your feelings as a guide.

If you feel confident and happy at the thought of leaving a marriage or relationship, your high vibrations will make you able to attract the right people, ideas and good situations. If you feel unsure about leaving, it's better to wait and see, taking more time before making the final decision.

And why is that? Because, without first lifting yourself from the heavy, low energies, you risk only attracting the same wounded feelings in your future relationships. If, on the other hand, you manage to lift your thoughts before making an important decision, you will be able to receive what the high-frequency stations are sending out: namely people, things and situations with good, light energies.

ASSIGNMENT 33

How can you think differently to attract the people you love into your life or, if you already have these people in your life, make them want to spend more time with you?

My Turn

From a young age, I quickly understood that one person would not be able to share all my different interests. That's why I operate with different groups of friends. With some of my friends, I do mainly fun stuff. With others, I do sporty things; a few, I travel with; and with some of my friends, I'm able to share philosophical and creative ideas.

Although it might be years between each time I see some of my friends, all of them are very important, as they all contribute, in one way or another, to shaping and inspiring me. Some of my friends are female, some male.

I have always had male friends, which wouldn't have worked out if my husband had been jealous. But luckily that's not the case, as he trusts me and I trust him.

My husband and I spend a lot of time apart, but, when we are together, we are very close. Because I am able to enjoy my own company, I'm seldom dependent on anybody else to make me happy. This is a great advantage in the life I've chosen to live. However, I believe it's not just important for me, but for most people. By having a good relationship with ourselves, we feel independent, which gives us a great feeling of freedom.

Nevertheless, moving around the way I do, I have to admit that I miss spending time with my family and friends. Lately I've been thinking through this issue to see if I can change my focus.

I'm rarely bored, but, if I am, I get creative and new stories or other creative projects begin to take shape. Therefore, it's good for me to be alone for some periods of time. The challenge is that I don't get enough outlets for my social needs with the lifestyle I have chosen to live.

By changing the way I look at my situation, I have begun to see how lucky I am to not only have friends and family in Norway, but also in Africa, the United States, Europe and Asia. With Facebook and Skype, we can keep in touch despite long distances. Actually, it is only up to me to make contact, as there is nothing that prevents me from writing or calling those whom I love.

I have felt a little frustrated lately, especially since I have not had the opportunity to talk to my sons and my parents in the same way as before. At the same time, this experience has given me the opportunity to practise consciously shifting my focus every time I observe that my mood and energy have started to sink. I have finally begun to understand that it is the quality and not the quantity of the time I spend with my family and friends that is important.

With my new awareness of what drives me and what makes me happy, I have seen that I need to be uprooted once in a while. My time in Ethiopia has again shown me how important it is to trust that my inner being will take me where it is best for me to be at all times. Had I decided to stay at home, I would not have had the opportunity to write this guide and I would not have been able to go on this self-development journey with myself or with you, and I really doubt I would have been as happy as I am now.

Your Turn

If you are struggling in any of your relationships, it might be good to invest some time working on them using the suggestions above. You can also visualise how you'd like your future relationships to be and give thanks to the people who surround you at the moment. If you really don't like the people who are around you, you can try to remove yourself from them.

Whatever you choose to believe or do, heightening your vibrations will make it much easier to attract the people you'd like to share your life with. Remember that you must be a match to what you want to attract, as you can't attract something or someone who vibrates in the high frequencies if your feelings are in the basement.

MANTRA: I see the value of both good and bad relationships and understand that I attract what I match. I will become more conscious in lifting myself up and vibrating in the high frequencies before I establish new relationships.

—That's it for now

NEXT TIME:

- Visualising your dream life
- Action steps towards your dream
- Time for relaxation and trust

TWELFTH JOURNEY TOGETHER

CONCRETISE YOUR DREAM

We are now nearing the end of our journey together and it's time to look into your dream and make it specific. Fleshing it out by being able to see, hear, smell and even feel your dream, as if it has already materialised, is a great way to start enjoying your dream even long before it has come into being.

Your insight into how energy can take different forms and respond to your thoughts, feelings and visualisations will give you the confidence that all dreams are achievable. The stronger your focus is on the dream, the faster it will materialise.

Being able to enjoy one piece of your dream at a time must be the goal, though. You don't want everything right this minute. If you don't spread it out, you won't be able to enjoy it. It would be like having to eat the whole cake at once and having nothing for tomorrow. However, **if the realisation of your dream is spread out, you can enjoy every moment.**

By talking to yourself in this way, you will feel relaxed in the knowledge that everything will unfold naturally. There is no reason to stress or panic. If you do, you just close the door to your dream.

ASSIGNMENT 34

See your dream in detail. Start to feel what it is like to live in this dream, as if you were pregnant with your "dream baby."

Remember, we live in the perspective of eternity, so, even if you're old or dying, there's no reason to stop dreaming.

My Turn

My dream had already started when I was still a child. I wanted to travel the world, live in Africa and write. Looking back, I can see how naturally everything has unfolded.

My life has followed a thread that constantly leads me towards my dreams and goals, and this has brought me many challenging situations to learn from. Sometimes, I have chosen to listen to my feelings, and sometimes I haven't and thus things have taken longer. Even though my dream has taken time to materialise, I can see that I needed every experience to be right where I am today.

If I had married one of my first boyfriends, I doubt that I would have managed to live out my dream. However, I have chosen to believe that the Source knew what I wanted from this lifetime and worked it all out for me.

I might not have started to write if it had not been for the shocking news that my brother was on the brink of suicide before he chose to stop his addiction. My first novel, *Same Mother, Same Father*, helped me process the shock. This experience was also the origin of my favourite mantra: "Nothing is so bad that it's not good for something."

If I hadn't chosen to move to Africa when I got the chance, I don't think I would have had the time and mental surplus to write my first novel so early in life. If I had instead taken a full-time job, while also dealing with two toddlers and having no help in the house, I would probably have had little energy left for writing. By following my feelings and accepting the challenges of traveling, I have slowly but surely moved towards my dream of writing.

The novel *Same Mother, Same Father* was hand-written, as we seldom had electricity in The Gambia. It was six-hundred pages long and not very good, but, from then on, I knew I was capable of finishing a novel and that no other activity could make me happier. Now, when I write, I just need the urge and then the words will flow out of me without my interference, as my inner being will take care of the content. If I get worried that I will not be able to finish my work, no words will come out of me until I again manage to relax.

Your Turn

Take your dream and get charged by it. Collect pictures of your dream and use as much spare time as you have to flesh it out in your mind. And don't stop until you feel the joy of knowing that exactly where you are now is, in fact, the best starting point for the journey towards your dream.

If you manage to enjoy the idea of being on your way to the dream without seeing signs that the dream is being materialised, you can expect a lot of good and you will feel good while waiting.

> **MANTRA:** The dream gives me direction for my own growth and development.

ACTION STEPS

The Source is capable of unfolding our dream; we need only trust and relax to get ourselves into a receptive mood. However, the people of this world are so action-oriented that sometimes, relaxing feels unnatural to us. In this case, we can make a plan and break it down into action steps without taking away our belief that the Source will deliver.

Even when a disaster comes your way, you know by now that it can bring just what you need in the wake of it and that there's no reason to worry or get upset. Following your bliss and impulses, using your feelings as a guiding system, is a great path because your inner being will tell you when to act in order to reach your dream. So, if you enjoy taking action, then there's no harm in doing so.

However, if you see that you're meeting one obstacle after another, it's time to find your happy place before continuing, and the same applies when you feel stressed. Stress is just a sign that you have started to swim upstream, holding your cork underwater. By letting go of the cork and turning onto your back and relaxing, you are back on your happy journey downstream again.

To take action steps means that you break down your goal into several action steps that lead to your goal. If you, for example, would like to travel around South America for a year, say in two years' time, then this journey is the big goal, and the two years, your timeline. The action steps are all the things you need to do before you can climb aboard the vehicle that will take you to your destination, things like checking travel prices, making a budget, saving money, learning the language, getting leave from school or work, buying your ticket, etc.

If you make sure your feelings are up to speed with every step of your dream, you can be certain to reach your goal, no matter how incredible your dream is. However, your goal might take a bit longer to materialise than you first imagined. If it takes longer before you can travel, you can be sure you are not yet a match to your dream. Trusting and knowing that everything will unfold at the right time is your best option, as, if you get stressed, angry or very disappointed, nothing good will happen until you are again able to get up to speed with what is delivered at the high vibrations.

ASSIGNMENT 35

Make a goal and break it down into realistic action steps. Keep your vibrations up by using meditation, gratitude and visualisation.

My Turn

Leaving college, I had a big dream of working in the United States as an au pair for a year. I was happy and very eager about finally being able to experience the country in which most of my favourite movies were made.

Everything had worked out smoothly; the only thing missing for me to be able to travel was to finalise my visa process. Two of my friends from school were also going, but they had already gotten their visas. Just before it was time for us to leave, I was asked to send some more documentation to the visa section. I didn't have it, and it stopped me from leaving.

I was very disappointed, especially since I was the one who had organised this opportunity for my friends. It took me some time to get up to speed with myself again and, when I did, I met "the boyfriend of my life," who's now my husband. Four years later, my husband and I went to the United States together and had a fantastic time studying and traveling all over the country. The interesting part of the story is that it turned out that I had a much more exciting experience in the States on this later trip than my friends had working as au pairs.

This just goes to show that sometimes we do not know the best timing for our desires to happen. Leaving it up to the Source to decide, we don't need to become so disappointed.

Now, when I make goals for myself, I still set a deadline for when I'd like things to happen, although, in my mind, I make it tentative so as to allow myself a bit of slack, as I know by now that the deadline I set might not have the right timing. Also, when I set action steps, I analyse how realistic I believe they are.

One of my goals is to publish a bestseller. So as not to be too disappointed, I've given myself a lifetime to achieve this goal, although it might take even longer … Nevertheless, by being too modest and not believing in my own inner being, I might get nowhere. If my wish is strong and I keep my vibrations high, I believe I can make it. To help me relax and have fun with my goal, I now call all my writing projects "My Bestseller."

In primary school, I often struggled to understand my homework because of my poor reading skills. When I was on the verge of giving up, my dad said, "Don't hide your light under a bushel, Nina! If others can do it, you can do it too." Dad sat down and finally taught me to see the difference between a 'b,' 'd' and 'p'. ('B' has a stomach, 'd' has a butt and 'p' has a neck.) My father's words: "If anyone else can do it, you can do it too," have since become one of my favourite mantras. If I want something badly enough and decide to believe in it by lifting my spirits, I can achieve all I decide to achieve, although I won't receive my desire before I am a match to it.

My husband calls me "The famous to be" ... and he has called me that for almost thirty-five years. I call myself "The late bloomer." Either way, if there is life, there is hope, and there is always life. Thus, there is no reason to despair, even if the dream takes time to materialise.

However, this requires that we are able to see the dream and our life in the perspective of eternity. Having said that, the stronger our focus and the better match we are for our dream, the sooner our dream will come true. Vibrating high can nevertheless be challenging and easy to forget in between, but practice makes you a master.

Your Turn

1. Take your dream or another goal and become aware of why you want to achieve it.

2. Put words to the feelings that achieving your dream will create in you: "trust," "energy," "understanding," "knowledge," "wisdom," "enthusiasm," "fascination," "happiness," "confidence," "tenderness," "love," "hope," "self-worth," "passion," "creativity," "dignity," "pride," "invincibility," "victory," "immortality," "gratitude," "freedom," etc. Spend some time on each feeling and register how your body responds.

   See also if you find these feelings present in your life today. If so, become aware of what you should focus on in your day-to-day life. The more you are able to have these feelings today, the more you will attract the same feelings in the future. By choosing happy thoughts, you choose happy feelings. This is the key to all creations.

3. Visualise the dream to the smallest detail. Use the time needed to enter your dream every day and get to know how it feels to be there. At the same time, be aware that your dream will change and evolve the more you focus on it.

4. Follow your own inspiration and impulse to act.

5. Remember that you must believe that your dream is achievable.

6. Keep your vibrations as high as possible using the tools you have learned.

> **MANTRA:** In any case, we all move forward. However, we are all given the freedom to choose how fast we wish to move.

TIME FOR RELAXATION AND TRUST

When you see that your timing is not right and you stumble and fall over and over again, take time out and start meditating or use your other tools. Giving yourself time to relax, being playful and having fun are the best solutions at moments like this, as a relaxed attitude will raise your vibrations. While taking your focus away from your goal, trust that you will feel the urge or impulse to act when the time is right; don't rush it.

Soothing works much better than banging your head against the wall, as beating will take you nowhere. Tell yourself that you have simply hit an obstacle and that there is always a way around it. If you can't see a way around the obstacle, take another route. The most important thing is to relax and trust that your desire is already waiting for you in the Vortex and that all you have to do to get yourself into a receptive mood is to heighten your vibrations.

Some people raise their vibrations by working hard. If you love to be active, it's still a good idea to take a break when you see that you are banging your head against the wall. It's easier to view your situation when you get a bit of distance. Another reason to stop and change focus is, as mentioned earlier, that life consists of many aspects, such as self-development, economy, work, social life, family, leisure and spirituality. If you do not find a balance between all the different aspects of life, it's harder to feel good. Nevertheless, it is useful to remember that you go in and out of balance.

At times, you can work very hard in one area. If you see that you are in a good flow where the timing is good, things are going well and you feel energetic and happy, there is no need to stop. But if you feel the opposite, tired and worn out, it's a good idea to stop and find something that makes you happy. Because the feeling of joy is the source of energy and inspiration.

If your goal is to get away from a job, a situation or a lifestyle that you really dislike, sit down and list all the things in your life that you like and keep your focus there. As soon as you have some time for yourself, visualise the life you desire in detail until you really feel that you are living that life. Then start laying a plan for how you can move towards your dream step by step. Remember, you must trust that your inner being will give you inspiration and impulses to act in the right places so the dream can be yours.

ASSIGNMENT 36

Practise monitoring your feelings. Consider why you have chosen this particular dream or goal. Ask yourself what motivates you. Perhaps you need a better attitude or a more positive focus, or maybe your goal is not inspiring enough. In other words, get to know yourself and your feelings. However, if you feel passionate and excited about your dream or goal, you know you're on the right track.

My Turn

I've been rejected so often in my life that it's a bit bizarre that I didn't give up a long, long time ago. For the first five novels I wrote, I felt devastated by each and every rejection I received. Now, however, I'm so used to it that I feel it's just a part of the game. "Rome wasn't built in a day," as they say. That is usually true for our dreams too.

For every mistake I make, I learn something new and, as long as I love what I'm doing, I don't see any reason to stop trying. Being happy, changing and growing to help the universe expand is my main goal. If I'm not going to write "My Bestseller" in this life, I have plenty of lifetimes ahead of me to give it another try. With this attitude, it doesn't matter anymore when my dream will come true. Being in a good process has become more important to me than reaching goals.

Abraham says that, if the aim of a journey is to reach the destination, there is no point of going out on a journey. **If the focus is on the end, you will not be able to enjoy the journey itself and you might as well have stayed at home.**

Your Turn

If you can look at life as a journey or a game where you get better for each level you master and where the goal is not to finish the game but to enjoy your own learning and growth, no resistance will be able to take your courage away from you.

None of us will manage to have such a positive focus on life all the time, but when you see that you are banging your head against the wall and are unable to lift yourself to the next level, you can stop what you are doing and choose to see life as a game or a journey. Looking at life as a journey, you see that you need to enjoy your experiences and not just focus on finishing or reaching a goal. If you are most focused on reaching the end and get irritated when the journey or game takes too long, you simply don't understand the purpose of life. If you have not understood the purpose of life, it's incredibly difficult to steer life in the direction you want to go.

Abraham Hicks says we have seventeen seconds before a vibration will start to materialise and give us feedback. This means you can get annoyed and frustrated, happy and excited for sixteen seconds without any consequence, but in the seventeenth second your feelings will be recorded and will, at one point, give you a response that matches your focus. Being disappointed, irritated and angry for a long time is therefore not a wise choice.

By getting used to feeling good, you'll soon be hooked on the feeling that these high vibrations give. This means that your body will quickly tell you when your feelings are dropping and you will start longing for the good feelings. As you get used to monitoring your feelings, seventeen seconds can sometimes be enough to change your mind and choose a higher vibration.

Your last challenge on this self-awareness journey will therefore be to practise monitoring your feelings.

Pick a time every day to monitor your feelings and do this exercise for as long as you need to. You don't have to know the details of your thoughts, only how you feel. If you feel very good, you know that the gap between yourself and your inner being is small and you are on the right track. The purpose of this exercise is to learn to take conscious control of your life and steer it in the direction you want. You will not avoid getting on to bumpy roads but you now have a tool similar to a GPS, which will take you back on a smooth road again as soon as you choose to follow the guidance that your feelings give you.

To be able to listen to your inner being though, you will need to practise. If you can't make it, it's not the end of the world. You just have to spend more time in the lower vibrations and take the consequences of your own creation of situations and people, which are not as much fun as those you'll find in the higher vibrations.

By now, however, you know that being able to relax when life sucks will heighten your vibrations much more quickly. If you can also see your pain and obstacles as just another downhill on the road to where you have decided to go, and decide that you don't need to make a long stopover at this spot, you will soon be able to consciously steer your life in the right direction and with the speed you want to go.

Changing the way you see yourself and the world is still a choice you have to make for yourself, as nobody will force you. The same goes for being willing to take the time to look into what you believe and how you can believe differently to make yourself feel good. You know by now that we are all given the freedom to choose when we want to move forward with our lives.

MANTRA: If I see life in the perspective of eternity, nothing is urgent. As soon as I remember to use my tools and am able to see my situation from a positive perspective, I am back on track towards my dream.

THE END OF OUR JOURNEY TOGETHER

CHECK YOUR GROWTH AND SOAR

If you have managed to do all your assignments and have come this far on your journey to self-discovery, I'm sure you are now able to see a tremendous change and growth in your life, and you'll definitely have a reason to celebrate! **Hip hip, hooray!**

• • •

Now it's time to read through your journal and reflect on your growth. Use a thirteenth month/week on this journey. Read carefully through your workbook and revisit the main points of your newly acquired insight. It will be satisfying to notice, in black and white, your own inner growth and change throughout our journey together.

You might not have been able to materialise or manifest your dream yet, but you should now know what you want from life and how to get there. You should also be able to relax and trust that your desire is already waiting for you in the higher vibrations.

By knowing that nobody is perfect, you no longer have to beat yourself up when life sucks, as contrast is needed to create new desires and new growth to make planet Earth evolve. You also know that you don't have to let these periods of contrast be painful or prolonged, but instead you can use them as a warning that you are on the wrong course.

Longing for happiness is what makes us develop and change. By using your feelings as a guide on your life journey, you now know that you can't go wrong and you will never be done, as your life will never stop evolving. If you don't reach your goals in this life, there will be plenty of opportunities later.

By consciously choosing a better way to see your situation, you now also know how to feel good in almost every situation in life, even if the situation is not as good as you had imagined. You have learned to do this by using your own mantra.

Through your meditation and gratitude lists, you are now also able to come into direct contact with your inner guide and the Source, as you know that you just need to choose to vibrate at the high energy frequencies to be able to listen to your inner being. You also remember that we are all part of the Source, and that everything in this world is energy that takes shape through our own thoughts, feelings and visualisations.

Furthermore, you know that you will not manage to stay up in the high vibrations for a long period at a time. Should you want to get back to the high frequencies again, you know that you have your own inner guide, which sends directions through your feelings.

Now that you have become familiar with your inner being, you will no longer need this guide to help you find your way to your dream life, as you have come to the place on our journey where you are able to practise raising your vibrations on your own. You have the tools you need and you know how to use them.

Now it's time to take the last leap into freedom by setting yourself in receiving mode so you can finally live a life that is really worth living. Go out on the edge of your own new conscious "thought base" and stretch your arms.

Are you ready to take the last, *big* step out into freedom?

Close your eyes and imagine you are flying in the direction of your dream, using your inner guide. As soon as you manage to feel the incredible freedom of knowing that you have your own built-in GPS and also manage to love yourself, your inner being and the world around you, nothing but you yourself can stop you from living the life you want.

Now that there is nothing that is preventing you, set yourself free and let your feelings guide you to the destination of your dreams!

This is the end of our journey together. However, it's also the beginning of your dream of "A Life Worth Living," so please enjoy your starting point of a new, exciting, fun and more meaningful life and try the best you can to make the most out of it! If you have done all your assignments, you should be able to enjoy both your ups and downs in the spiral of life towards change and expansion, while living the life you yourself think is worth living.

That's it: you made it.

CONGRATULATIONS!

THE WAY FORWARD

If you should feel lost at any stage of your life, you can come back to this guide again, as it's very easy to forget our purpose in life and to feel lost. You can also do as I do and listen to Abraham Hicks when you feel the need to be reminded who you really are and that seeking happiness and high vibrations is your only mission on planet Earth.

Abraham is a group consciousness from the non-physical who uses Esther Hicks to convey insights to people who want answers to their questions about life. This is the only source of knowledge and wisdom my inner being resonates with, and maybe it also resonates with you by now.

At the back of the book, you will find a link from which you can choose from hundreds of meetings with Abraham on different subjects, depending on what you want to learn about. When your mood drops, you can also check out other "Feel Good" videos on the website.

If you find it difficult to do this journey on your own, go to the "Forum for Change" on **www.a-life-worth-living.org/forum/** and see if you can set up a group or just chat with some like-minded people. It is important to keep the discussion positive using the tools that are given in this guide in order to focus on the solutions rather than the problems. You can also use this guide together with a coach, a psychologist, family or a friend, or at school, at a rehab centre or for couple's therapy. You can even use the workbook and this guide to set up a local group for people who really want change.

As soon as you discover that you are not dependent on other people around you to behave the way you want, or that the situation you are in right now does not necessarily have to be good for you to feel well, then you have come a long way on the journey to a life of freedom. In addition, you give yourself the privilege of experiencing unconditional love.

Unconditional love is something that very few people get the pleasure of experiencing, as we are trained to believe that love is something that is given to us by other people and not something we can deliberately choose to give to ourselves, regardless of anyone else.

The source of love lies within you, not outside. The Source is pouring its love to you all the time. When you choose not to listen to your inner being but are fully focused on your external circumstances, you close the door to your inner source of love and you feel lonely and abandoned. This guide has been designed to teach you how to open up this immense flow of unconditional love from the Source through the use of mainly three types of tools. These are now your tools. But it will be up to you if you want to use them.

Some give the tool kit to people who are in real need; others will put it down in the basement and wait for the next time they slide all the way down to the bottom of their scale of emotions before they choose to retrieve it again. Only a few will see the benefit of working through the workbook and learn how to use the tools so that they can begin to live their dreams in the lives they live here and now.

We are all at different levels in the game of our life's journey, so it is quite natural that we will make different choices. If you have decided to work through the workbook, start immediately. If you wait for another day, you will lose the momentum you've already built up. It will then be harder to take yourself to the unknown heights where your dreams are just waiting to be signed out by you.

THANK YOU!

Thank you so much for taking the time to go on this journey together with me. I really appreciate it! Hopefully it has been as much an eye-opener for you as it has been for me.

A big "thanks" goes to all the people who have touched my life in one way or another; without you, I would not have been able to write this guide. I'm really so, so grateful!

Special thanks go to my husband, my two sons, and their girlfriends, who inspired me to write this guide. Without their encouragement, I doubt that I would have started this project.

I am also grateful for all the help I received from my editor, Amber Hatch, my beautiful and talented proofreaders, Sophie Hazel and Bethany Davis but also for all the advice and technical help from my dear husband and incredibly patient, knowledgeable and kind son, Torstein. Had it not been for their help, I'm afraid that this product would not have the same quality.

I wish you all the best on your life journey and your way forward! Remember, you can never go wrong and you can never get it done. Nevertheless, it's all up to yourself how fun you choose to make your journey.